ST. MARY'S COLLEGE OF MARYLAND LIBRARY
ST. MARY'S CITY, MARYLAND

CHE: A PERMANENT TRAGEDY

RANDOM TARGETS

MATIJA BEĆKOVIĆ & DUŠAN RADOVIĆ

Translated by Drenka Willen

MATIJA BEĆKOVIĆ

CHE: A PERMANENT TRAGEDY

New York   Harcourt Brace Jovanovich, Inc.

RANDOM TARGETS

Copyright © 1970 by Harcourt Brace Jovanovich, Inc. All rights reserved. No part of this publication may be reproduced or transmitted in any form or by any means, electronic or mechanical, including photocopy, recording, or any information storage and retrieval system, without permission in writing from the publisher.

First edition

ISBN 0–15–117025–8

Library of Congress Catalog Card Number: 76-126525

Printed in the United States of America

PUBLISHER'S NOTE

Matija Bećković and Dušan Radović are younger spokesmen of that postwar European literary generation that believes the human condition is essentially a state of exile, in which man is alienated from the familiar assumptions of the past and cannot subscribe to illusions that promise something better for the future. Man in his marginal and contingent condition, they believe, feels himself to be superfluous, *de trop*. His experience is one of profound anxiety, of "metaphysical anguish."

This sense of spiritual distress found its most eloquent expression in the postwar writings of Camus, who saw man as a stranger "in a universe that is suddenly deprived of illusions and of light . . . deprived of a lost homeland as much as he lacks the hope of a promised land to come." He described this feeling of separation and hopelessness as the state of absurdity—a sense of the incongruity of one's own existence. Perhaps nowhere in the postwar world is a similar sense of displacement, of separation from the past, felt more deeply than in Eastern Europe and particularly in Yugoslavia, the "homeland" of Radović and Bećković. Yugoslavia is a country that has long suffered a fragmentation and divisiveness amongst its peoples. Its failure to achieve a unified and harmonious sense of identity is a political dilemma. As a country that emerged from a ravaging and brutalizing war only to find itself defined—indeed established—by a new political ideology, the very precariousness of life and absence of any historical certainty or moral commonality would necessarily have a sobering effect on its artists. It has had, understandably, precisely that effect on the two playwrights who wrote *Che: A Permanent Tragedy*. This is a play that just as surely as Beckett's *Waiting for Godot* tells us that we are not going anywhere, that life is ludicrous, and that the signposts pointing to a route of progress offer no solutions. There is a telling line in the play that says

We are confronted with a blank wall.
The show is over. . . .

There was a time, according to Bećković and Radović, when writers were prophets and visionaries whose perceptions of the world based on a sense of rationality and order could give a sense of direction and bring the future into perspective with the present. But the role of seer is no longer possible or desirable, for artists now do not "have the confidence to make esthetic judgments about the fundamental questions concerning their destiny." The role of the modern writer, we are told by Bećković and Radović, is to state "what twentieth-century man feels and thinks" and to offer a serious dialogue about what is immediate and real. And this should be done in a language that avoids embellishment or self-conscious verbalism or private introspection. Today, the literary weapons left to the writer who is intolerant of deception and illusion are irony, cynicism, and humor. These weapons are used by Matija Bećković brilliantly in his epigrammatic essays that form the latter part of this book. Not since the Polish writer Leć has wit been employed so practically against nonsense.

Bećković and Radović are representative of the contemporary esthetic sensibility. In an age that has seen a renaissance of the cinematic arts and the flowering of *cinéma vérité* and the documentary film, they reveal an affinity to that medium which more than any other can register a "reality" that is stripped of delusion and fantasy and façade.

Edith Hamilton once wrote that the ancient Greeks had achieved a great society because they told no "vital lies." Matija Bećković in his essays, and with Dušan Radović in *Che,* questions modern society's vital lies—those organizations, movements, and personal roles that have traditionally offered solutions for the ills of mankind—religion, the army, the *avant-garde,* reformers, workers, intellectuals, heroes. These authors are authentic witnesses of the future as present.

CHE: A PERMANENT TRAGEDY

Scene I

The stage tilts slightly downward toward the audience. A dozen or so crosses may be seen in the semidark as the curtain rises. The ACTORS lie under the crosses. THE MAN WITH THE CROSS enters from right. HE moves slowly, glances around wondering to whom HE should speak. Finally HE turns to the audience.

    THE MAN WITH THE CROSS
    Who asked for this?
    Which one of you asked for this cross?

HE waits for a reply.
HE looks around.

    Somebody *did* ask for this cross!

HE waits again.
Getting no reply, HE shrugs and exits.
Music.
One cross ascends to heaven.
THE FRIGHTENED MAN rises,
turns to the audience.

THE FRIGHTENED MAN

I want to live. I'm not guilty.
I'm not complaining. I have
everything I need. Let me live.
What do I know about it? Nothing.
I've got problems enough of my own.
Just pay no attention to me.
I don't deserve it. I simply
want—at any price and under
any circumstances—to live.
With no rights and no future.
I'm here by accident.
I agree with you completely.
I'm afraid. I don't deserve
any better life than what I've got.
Don't fight—not for me. I
want to live. Nobody asked me.
I never said a thing. I am
alone—no friends, nobody.
I don't want to die. I want to live.
Leave me alone. I'll die alone.
I love people—all people.
I'm not accusing anybody.
I am a coward—a member
of nothing, a null.
My life is dull. I'm not in
anybody's way. Take all I've got.
I need nothing. Just leave me
my life. I'll never get another
chance to live—if I don't live now.

THE FRIGHTENED MAN steps back
a few paces, then sits down in the
semidark. Another cross
ascends to heaven.
THE BITTER MAN gets to his feet,
comes downstage.

           THE BITTER MAN
        I hate life. I hate facts.
        Truth is cruel.
        Lie to me. Only tell me that
        everything is beautiful.
        I'm sick of proofs, numb to arguments.
        Science is an enemy of progress.
        Take me where I can dream.
        I can't see, I can't hear,
        I don't know a thing.
        Save me from the truth.
        This sort of life's a bore.
        Sing to me about the future.
        My patience has run out;
        time's run out, too.
        What say we go see that film
        about the meaning of it all!
        Rescue me. I'm drowning,
        going under in a swamp of
        reality—the real muck.
        If it's the quickest way out,
        kill me.

Take me beyond life, outside of life.
I had no choice. I was forced
into this world—the wrong world.
This is no life for me.
I've tasted everything.
We were cheated. Nothing
here's proportioned to man.
It's a hostile world we live in.
Let's clear out before they eat us alive.
There must be more to life than this.
Where is the life we dreamed about?
Where's all that happiness you promised us?

THE BITTER MAN steps back.
Another cross flies up to heaven.
THE GIRL rises and comes
down toward the audience.

    THE GIRL
I understand why the guilty must die.
They deserve their punishment. They die willingly.
But why should an innocent man die—
a man who did no evil,
who obeyed and worked hard and studied,
thinking that sometime all this would be of some use?

I thought the reason death existed
was so we could tell
the sinners from the innocent.

If it's all the same, everything's worthless.
What's the point of living just in order to die?
Whoever dies deserves death.
The harshest punishment seeks out guilt.

If there are any advantages in death
I don't know what they are.
There's no reason why I should die.
I'm innocent.
The innocent have no reason to die.
They should live forever.
They have a perfect right to.
And not in heaven, either, but on earth—
where they were born, where they belong.
The fact that up till now nobody
has lived forever is probably
proof that there's never been
a single innocent on earth.
Maybe, though, there *is* one
who's been living in some secret place
for centuries—underground and unregistered—
just breathing and seeing and waiting for
an innocent friend to come and talk to him.

THE GIRL steps back.
Music.
The remaining crosses ascend
heavenward together.
The ACTORS rise.
The space grows a bit brighter.
THE LIFE-LOVING MAN comes downstage.

THE LIFE-LOVING MAN
The sun, the earth, springtime and water—
these things belong to everyone.
They're ours by birthright.
You can't possibly get more
than you've already got.
How can you be more equal
than anybody else, when each of you has got
only two legs, two arms,
one heart, one life?
What brand of justice can give you more?
Man's been given all he needs.
Everybody's lot should be improved—yes,
but only as much as each can do
for himself. Freedom and justice?
They're not for all. It's nations
that deal in things like freedom and justice
and truth.
And there's never been enough to go around.

THE LIFE-LOVING MAN steps back.
THE WOMAN struts forward.

THE WOMAN
What is *real* life?
Isn't every life *real*?
Doesn't everybody lead his own *real* life?
Has anybody managed to yet?
Who? Whose life, for example?
Who decides which life is *real*?
Are all *real* lives the same?

Does the person who doesn't lead one
deserve to live?
Is one allowed to kill
in the name of *real* life?
Why should anybody want to live
any other sort of life
than the *real* life?
Do *real* livers die, too?
What is it in life that isn't life?
Do you think man's good enough
for the *real* life?
How do you convince man
to live otherwise?

As THE WOMAN concludes,
THE LIFE-LOVING MAN steps forward.

THE LIFE-LOVING MAN
Life's only a small theft snatched
from eternal death.
One must live.
Of all the billions who have ever lived
or will live—only we are alive.
One must enjoy life.
Those who don't know how to live,
how to enjoy life—they're a denial
of life's affirmation.
If people hate life, it's because
they're defective.
If they seek death, it's because
they prefer it.

They long for a justice that never was,
for a dream of honesty,
for a fairy-tale freedom.
They no longer live.
They dream.

As THE LIFE-LOVING MAN steps back,
THE MAN IN UNIFORM steps forward.

    THE MAN IN UNIFORM
I wonder why there have been so many heroes
around lately. Nobody's satisfied. Nobody's
got enough.
You were hungry. What did you do?
Instead of stuffing yourselves, you turned
being hungry into a tragic, masochistic play.
It bothered you that people weren't hungry
any more
after they'd eaten. Wars don't cure poverty.
No freedom ever brought more bread.
It takes a nation twenty years after a war
to live as well as it did before.
The poor don't get rich by defeating the rich.
If the ugly people rise against the beautiful,
and win, will they be any prettier than they
were before?
Or will there no longer be any beautiful people?
I have more faith in medicine
than in politics, thank you.

The poor are most numerous where
the poor have won.
The poor man gains nothing when he wins.
He just loses hope.

THE SECOND MAN IN UNIFORM
joins HIM.

SECOND MAN IN UNIFORM
You thought you were unhappy,
but you were hungry.
You thought you'd been robbed of your rights.
In fact you were impotent.
You thought you were suffering an injustice,
but you had a toothache.
You thought you pitied others,
but you loved yourself.

Instead of eating,
you started to kill.
Instead of learning,
you began teaching others.
Instead of having your tooth pulled,
you started a revolution.
Instead of changing yourself,
you thought you'd change the world.

THE MAN WITH THE PROGRAM
joins THEM.

THE MAN WITH THE PROGRAM
Here's *my* program. I've never
come across a better one. Listen!
Sirloin steak, filet mignon,
Wiener schnitzel, braised calf's brains,
pot roast and scallops sauté.
There'll be a twenty-minute wait, that's all.
Take your pick. You'll get it served
on a silver platter.
Excuse me.
I just don't know of any more solid promise
or of any future as near as this one.
And I'm positive nobody ever
promised more to the hungry.
There's a minor dilemma, of course.
Which will it be—
calf's brains or filet mignon?
Pot roast or sirloin?
Broadcast this program throughout the world.
I count on receiving overwhelming support.

When THE MAN WITH THE PROGRAM
concludes his speech, ALL stand—
wherever THEY happen to be standing
—and freeze, dumfounded.
Pause. Loud music.
THE MAN WITH THE CROSS enters
from the left this time. HE pauses.
THE OTHERS catch sight of HIM and
silently vanish.

Alone, THE MAN WITH THE CROSS
turns to the audience.

>THE MAN WITH THE CROSS
>Well, here it is. Somebody phoned and asked
>me to bring this cross here. Which of you called?
>Who needs the cross? Well?

HE stands still, waiting for a reply.
None comes. HE shrugs and exits
right. As soon as HE has left, a mob
of colorfully dressed DEMONSTRATORS
rushes onstage carrying all sorts of
odds and ends: posters, chairs, lamps,
books, busts, candle holders, flower-
pots, bedsprings, water pitchers,
beach balls, dolls, etc. THEY sprint
across the stage, jump, scream, and
display whatever THEY're holding.
There are, in all, six DEMONSTRATORS
—five men, one woman.

>FIRST MAN
>Causes! In first-rate condition!
>Hardly used and no worse for the wear!
>Causes for sale! Causes!

>SECOND MAN
>Two idols here—idols for a song!
>Cut-rate prices! Absolutely free!

THE WOMAN
I train assassins.

THIRD MAN
Programs! Directions!
Road maps! Solutions!

FOURTH MAN
Hatred! For everything!

FIFTH MAN
Tickets here! Get your
tickets for history!

THE WOMAN
A thirst for freedom.

FOURTH MAN
A stock of screams guaranteed
to move absolutely everybody!

FIFTH MAN
An assortment of overlooked
historical facts!

FIRST MAN
I'd give my right hand for a just cause.

SECOND MAN
A genuine antique Latin saying—
two thousand years old.
Something about the victory
of justice.

THE WOMAN
Secrets! Secrets! Military secrets!

THIRD MAN
I expand, contract, abbreviate,
and otherwise edit political programs!

FOURTH MAN
I compose the most beautiful promises.

FIFTH MAN
A quick refresher course in
short cuts to Utopia!

THE WOMAN
I darn flags.

SECOND MAN
Statistics! Take your pick!

Two SERGEANTS, fighting over a flag,
rush into this confusion. The flag is

big, red, and its two sides are
bordered with spears.

        FIRST SERGEANT
        Give me that flag!

        SECOND SERGEANT
        Not on your life!

        FIRST SERGEANT
        But it's *ours!*

        SECOND SERGEANT
        Like hell it is! It's ours.

        FIRST SERGEANT
        Yours? You don't deserve . . .

        SECOND SERGEANT
        Some of our best comrades died for this flag.

        FIRST SERGEANT
        Y*our* comrades? They were ours.

        SECOND SERGEANT
        This flag stands for our struggle.

FIRST SERGEANT
Your struggle? *Ours*, you mean.

SECOND SERGEANT
We swore . . .

FIRST SERGEANT
So did we. . . .

SECOND SERGEANT
We'd rather *die* than . . .

FIRST SERGEANT
So would we.

SECOND SERGEANT
. . . rather die than give up our flag.

FIRST SERGEANT
Die under it then, but you can't live under it.

SECOND SERGEANT
We'll never surrender it. It's all we've got.

FIRST SERGEANT
If it's really all you've got, what do you need the flag for?

SECOND SERGEANT
First you steal all our ideals, and now you want our flag!

FIRST SERGEANT
This flag's the color of our blood.

SECOND SERGEANT
Your blood? *Ours!* You've betrayed this flag.

FIRST SERGEANT
Why don't you just calm down and come over to our side?

SECOND SERGEANT
Never! Not as long as your flag's the same as ours.

FIRST SERGEANT
Long live the flag of freedom!

SECOND SERGEANT
Your freedom? No. That's not what our flag stands for.

The two SERGEANTS run off.
The OTHERS continue hawking their wares.

THE WOMAN
A substitute for truth!

FIRST MAN
A cure for good memories!

SECOND MAN
Blueprints for a conspiracy!

FOURTH MAN
And plans for setting up a new government!

THE WOMAN
Pills to relieve acid indigestion.

FIFTH MAN
Mistakes for sale! Buy ours;
they're bound to be better than yours.

THIRD MAN
A cure for every injustice!

SECOND MAN
A handbook for revolutionaries!

WOMAN
How to become a leader—in just
one hundred easy lessons!

SECOND MAN
A wide selection of the most
beautiful futures you ever heard of.

FIRST MAN
Contact with the Center—
wherever that is.

THIRD MAN
Medals and decorations!
Pay in easy installments.

THE WOMAN
Hitler's letters to his mother!

FOURTH MAN
Stalin's letters to his daughter!

SECOND MAN
Fresh illusions!

FIFTH MAN
A cure for hunger!

THE WOMAN
Opium—opium for the masses!

THEY come to a sudden stop and fall silent.
Music. Cymbals.
The FIRST MAN gives a start, gets down on his knees, and puts an ear to the ground. HE listens for some time. The SECOND MAN walks over to HIM. HE watches the FIRST MAN. Though HE doesn't understand what's going on, HE also gets down on his knees and listens. From time to time, HE glances up in bewilderment at the FIRST MAN. The THIRD, FOURTH, FIFTH, and SIXTH MAN, and THE WOMAN follow suit. Music.
THEY listen, glance at each other, bewildered. While still down on their knees, THEY start talking.

          FIRST MAN
     Did you hear that?

          ALL
     No!

          FIRST MAN
     Listen. . . .

THEY all listen.

FIRST MAN
The dead down there—they're rebelling.

THE WOMAN
I can't hear a thing.

THIRD MAN
I can.

SECOND MAN
Yes, they're shouting and wailing.

FIFTH MAN
What do they want?

FIRST MAN
They aren't happy.

FOURTH MAN
What are they unhappy about? Their death?

FIRST MAN
No, our lives.

HE listens. THEY listen, too.

FIRST MAN
They never stop talking. . . . They're asking, "What did we die for?"

THEY continue to listen. One by one THEY get angry and start beating the ground with their fists. THEY shout:

SECOND MAN
Quiet, down there. . . . What do you want?

THIRD MAN
You're suffocating us.

FOURTH MAN
We can't tell who's alive and who's dead!

THE WOMAN
Leave us alone!

FIRST MAN
You fools, let us live. . . .

SECOND MAN
We no longer need the authority of the dead. It's unbearable.

THE WOMAN
Shut up!

THEY listen.
Music intensifies.

FIRST MAN
They say we've betrayed them.

FIFTH MAN
No, they betrayed us.

THE WOMAN
We spend our whole lives straightening out their mistakes.

THIRD MAN
Idealists! Dreamers!

SECOND MAN
Demagogues! Dogmatists!

THE WOMAN
Enough! Calm down.

THEY listen. Music intensifies. THEY rise abruptly, one after the other. THEY stamp their feet; THEY shout

to deafen the music that grows
louder—the voices of the dead.

>   ALL
>   You are jealous of our lives.
>   It's so easy to be wise when you're dead.
>   Leave us alone.
>   When it comes to our problems, you're blind
>   as bats.
>   Stop your babble. You can't help us any more.
>   Quiet! That's enough.
>   Go to sleep. We are living your dreams.

Slowly THEY calm down.
Pause.
Two uniformed GRAVEDIGGERS enter.
Between them THEY carry a huge
beribboned wreath of artificial
flowers. The ACTORS help them lay
the wreath on the ground, then
arrange themselves around the
wreath like an honor guard. Music.
A funeral march.
The uniformed GRAVEDIGGERS exit
and return again lugging a pulpit and
a coat rack with six top hats dangling
from pegs or hooks. THEY put the
coat rack next to the pulpit. And a
glass of water on the pulpit. The
uniformed GRAVEDIGGERS leave. One
by one, the ACTORS go through the

following ritual: EACH goes up to the
coat rack, takes a top hat, puts it on,
stations himself behind the pulpit,
takes a sip of water, raises his top hat
and shouts a slogan.

    FIRST MAN
    We will never forget the fighters of March 13!

    SECOND MAN
    We will remain faithful to the victims of June 18!

    THIRD MAN
    We will remember those who fell on the tragic
    night of September 3!

    FOURTH MAN
    We will never repeat the Second of October!

    FIFTH MAN
    Long live the indomitable Sixth of November!

    THE WOMAN
    Let the flame of August 17, which blazed
    up again on December 2, continue to burn!

    FIRST MAN
    May the nights between February 1 and 16
    live in our hearts forever!

SECOND MAN
All glory to October 11!

THIRD MAN
May the bright light of June 59 never go out!

FOURTH MAN
The indelible images of May 34!

FIFTH MAN
Never will the enemy forget the bloody morning of January 6!

THE WOMAN
The echo of gunfire of March 15!

FIRST MAN
The torch of October 18!

SECOND MAN
The flames of July 3!

THIRD MAN
The storms of August 18!

FOURTH MAN
The stunning victory of April 1!

FIFTH MAN
The triumph of December 15!

THE WOMAN
The truth of the Seventh and the Sixth!

FIRST MAN
Long live our victories of the First,
the Sixteenth, and the Twenty-Seventh
of the month.

SECOND MAN
April 17—a red-letter day in our hearts
and calendars!

THIRD MAN
February 69—Farmers' Day!

FOURTH MAN
March 78—Ladies' Day!

The curtain starts to descend.
Following the applause of the
audience, or of a tape recorder, the
curtain goes up again, and THEY
continue their ritual.

FIFTH MAN
February 7 will be the third anniversary
of the glorious Third of October!

THE WOMAN
Praise be to the Eighth and the Fifth!

FIRST MAN
We must all learn from the example of
December 31!

SECOND MAN
Let us bow to the Nineteenth of March!

FOURTH MAN
And preserve the ideals of June 3.

FIFTH MAN
And remain faithful to the Nineteenth of April.

THE WOMAN
Let us warm ourselves with memories of
November 9.

FIRST MAN
And never betray the Fourth of October.

SECOND MAN
And always remember the Fifth of December.

THIRD MAN
Let us fight for the victory of January 1.

FOURTH MAN
The dawn of May!

FIFTH MAN
One morning in April!

THE WOMAN
That night in December!

SECOND MAN
The stars in July.

THIRD MAN
The September barricades!

FOURTH MAN
The red winter!

FIFTH MAN
The fruits of February!

FIRST MAN
Victorious spring!

ALL
Long live the First, the Second, the Third!
The Fourth, the Fifth, the Sixth! The Seventh,
the Eighth, the Ninth! The Tenth, the
Eleventh, the Twelfth of January, February,
March, April, May! June, July, August,
September! October, November, December!
And backward!

Curtain

Scene II

The curtain rises.
The background is decorated with slogans, unidentifiable portraits, flags, etc. Three microphones hang from the ceiling. THE WORKER enters the stands in front of one of the microphones. A noose drops down over the microphone. Seeing it, THE WORKER moves over to the next microphone. After HE has spoken two lines, a noose drops over the second microphone. Seeing it in the nick of time, HE crosses over to the third microphone. Again a noose falls. After delivering two more lines, THE WORKER comes downstage close to the audience.

>THE WORKER
>Some deliver speeches,
>some write books,
>some curse
>   —THE PEOPLE KNOW NOTHING ABOUT IT!
>The leader is chosen,
>songs are sung,
>medals distributed
>   —THE PEOPLE KNOW NOTHING ABOUT IT!
>Money is borrowed,
>agreements concluded,
>friends made

>   —THE PEOPLE KNOW NOTHING ABOUT IT!
> The future is planned—
> better lives for all,
> injustice banished
>   —THE PEOPLE KNOW NOTHING ABOUT IT!
> Mistakes are made,
> a new bunch takes over,
> there'll be no deviation
>   —THE PEOPLE KNOW NOTHING ABOUT IT!
> Somebody's plotting,
> the plot is discovered,
> many are beaten
>   —THE PEOPLE KNOW NOTHING ABOUT IT!
> A decision is made,
> we're going to be sent off to war,
> The cause is holy
>   —THE PEOPLE KNOW NOTHING ABOUT IT!

As THE WORKER concludes his speech, two MEN come up behind him. THEY grab him, then start tossing him back and forth between them. After torturing HIM, THEY throw him down on the floor.

FIRST MAN
Confess that you're free.

THE WORKER
I confess.

SECOND MAN
Confess that you're happy.

THE WORKER
I confess.

FIRST MAN
Confess that you love us.

THE WORKER
I confess.

SECOND MAN
Confess that we're equal.

THE WORKER
I confess.

FIRST MAN
Confess that everything's the way you want it.

THE WORKER
I confess.

SECOND MAN
What haven't you confessed yet?

THE WORKER
I don't know.

FIRST MAN
Confess that this is your victory.

THE WORKER
I confess.

SECOND MAN
Confess that you are our brother.

THE WORKER
I confess.

FIRST MAN
Did you confess you were happy?

THE WORKER
I don't know.

SECOND MAN
Confess!

THE WORKER
I confess.

FIRST MAN
Do you feel better now that you've confessed everything?

THE WORKER
I do.

SECOND MAN
Confess!

THE WORKER
I confess.

FIRST MAN
What do you say?

THE WORKER
Thank you.

The two MEN knock THE WORKER to
the ground, seize microphones and
address the audience.

FIRST MAN
Forgive us!
We are your *avant-garde*.
We represent—not your opinions—
but your own best interests.
We didn't ask you, because we don't care
what you opinions are.
What you think
is not in your own
best interests.

SECOND MAN
Forgive us!
We lied, lied to humanity.
We said you wanted it this way.
You've always resisted
what's good for you.
You've always been
a counterrevolutionary.
While we were busy solving your problems,
you were snoring in your bed.
You learn of your victories
from your local newspaper;
you gaze at pictures of unknown men
who were shot instead of you.

FIRST MAN
Forgive us!
We think, dream, and talk
in your name.
It was we, in fact,
who gave you your name
and your cause and your banner.
Didn't we prove to you
that you were hungry and exploited?
Foolish child, you can't see
beyond the end of your own nose.

SECOND MAN
Forgive us!
We are your eyes and your ears.

It is our sacred duty
to lead you to ultimate victory.
One way or another—don't worry—
we'll guide you to a better future.
You're deaf and blind,
so just leave it to us.
Leading others is our
assignment in life.
Forgive us!
We can't wait around until
you've all understood.
We don't have the time.

Music starts up—a march.
Four armed SOLDIERS enter. THEY
parade back and forth several times,
then come to attention in front of
the two MEN. The FIRST SOLDIER
then steps back and completes his
speech. The other three SOLDIERS
follow the same ritual, then THEY
regroup and, while slapping their
rifles into various positions, chant
the last nine slogans in unison.

        FIRST SOLDIER
There's nothing the bullet can't cure.
It takes care of a headache in no time.

SECOND SOLDIER
The last word in medical science, the bullet—
"world's most reliable pain killer."

THIRD SOLDIER
Nature's best remedy is the bullet—
"the tranquilizer with humanity."

FOURTH SOLDIER
No other cure will cure what a bullet can cure.
Sometimes there's no other way the patient
can be saved.

THEY go through a rifle drill.

ALL
The bullet is safe and quick.
The bullet's available to all.
The bullet's a time-honored remedy.
With a bullet you do it yourself.
The bullet's a popular pill.
One bullet per person will do.
There's no cheaper cure on the market.
Even here—in this country—
there are bullets for all.

The exercise over, THEY regroup,
wheel, and march offstage followed

by the two MEN. THE MAN WITH THE
CROSS enters. HE walks around looking for something or somebody, then
turns to the audience.

> THE MAN WITH THE CROSS
> Well, here's the cross! What happened?
> Look, who's going to pay for this cross?
> I made it for somebody. Now, whose cross
> is this? I make my living selling these things!

HE waits for a reply, gets none,
shrugs, and leaves. TWO MASKED MEN
appear on opposite sides of the stage.
THEY are cautious, shy, hesitant.
EACH hides behind a large portable
screen—poking his head out to speak,
then ducking back behind his screen.

> FIRST MASK
> All hail to them!

> SECOND MASK
> To hell with 'em!

> FIRST MASK
> The best!

SECOND MASK
The worst!

FIRST MASK
Invincible!

SECOND MASK
Whipped!

FIRST MASK
Indestructible!

SECOND MASK
Smashed!

FIRST MASK
Peace-loving!

SECOND MASK
Warmongers!

FIRST MASK
Absolutely sincere!

SECOND MASK
Consistently false!

FIRST MASK
Ours!

SECOND MASK
Yours!

FIRST MASK
Our hopes!

SECOND MASK
Your delusions!

FIRST MASK
Our mothers-in-law!

SECOND MASK
Your mothers-in-law!

FIRST MASK
But that's what *I* said!

SECOND MASK
You can have them!

THEY *stop, ducking behind their screens.* TWO MORE MASKED MEN *enter, hiding behind screens and peeking out from behind them as,* speaking their lines, THEY move back and forth across the stage.

> THIRD MASK
> Me? No future.
> —You? No apartment.

> FOURTH MASK
> Me? No job.
> —You? No food.

> THIRD MASK
> Me? No brains.
> —You? No head.

> FOURTH MASK
> Me? No plans.
> —You? No blanket.

> THIRD MASK
> Me? No skill.
> —You? No money.

> FOURTH MASK
> Me? No faith.
> —You? No dessert.

> THIRD MASK
> Me? No friends.
> —You? No feet.

FOURTH MASK
Me? No road.
—You? No car.

THIRD MASK
Me? Know nothing.

FOURTH MASK
Me? *Own* nothing.

THIRD MASK
Me?

FOURTH MASK
You.

THIRD MASK
You?

FOURTH MASK
Me.

THEY stop and duck back behind their screens.
TWO MORE MASKED MEN enter. THEY, too, hide behind screens. EACH waves a flag. THEY move back and forth, waving their flags and ducking in and out from behind their screens.

FIFTH MASK
Our best comrades died for this flag!

SIXTH MASK
So? What did you kill them for?

FIFTH MASK
Long live freedom!

SIXTH MASK
Long live *our* freedom!

FIFTH MASK
But there can't be two!
Freedom is indivisible.

SIXTH MASK
Keep your freedom.
We don't want any part of it.

FIFTH MASK
But ours is the only true freedom!
We'll liberate you!

SIXTH MASK
Help, comrades. They're stealing our flag!

THEY stop, ducking behind their
screens as a disheveled AGITATOR

rushes onstage. A noose is tied around his neck.
HE carries his own chair, climbing up on it each time HE shouts a slogan. HE addresses each screen in turn.

>AGITATOR
>Down with the villains!
>Let the sun of freedom shine forever!

>ALL
>Let it shine!

>AGITATOR
>Down with injustice!
>Long live freedom!

>ALL
>Long live freedom!

>AGITATOR
>I am an agitator! I start revolutions, expand frontiers, hold out new hopes! Well—why don't you string me up?

>ALL
>We have no orders!

AGITATOR
Then *ask* for orders!

ALL
We did. They wouldn't give us any.

AGITATOR
Why? Where did I slip up?
Where did I go wrong?

ALL
Don't worry. You haven't made
any mistakes so far.

AGITATOR
You can't be listening to me, then.
I say, down with the bloodthirsty monsters!
Down with tyrants!

ALL
Down with them!

AGITATOR
I hate Jews!

ALL
We hate Jews!

AGITATOR
But I kill Slavs!

ALL
So do we!

AGITATOR
Hang me. Please. I dream of the scaffold.

ALL
Why should we hang you?

AGITATOR
You've killed others for no good reason.

ALL
They deserved it.

AGITATOR
Well, what about me? Nobody's ever said what I'm saying now! Down with exploiters! Down with murderers! Down with the criminals!

ALL
We've heard that line before.
Give us something new.

AGITATOR
Kill me. I dream of the scaffold.
Just don't torture me.
I'm your worst enemy.
I am sincere.
Kill me because I'm sincere.

ALL
Come around tomorrow. We'll see.

AGITATOR
But I can't wait any longer.
I'll die before you've made up your minds.
The shame! Think of it—an agitator
dying a natural death.
But on the scaffold one catches
a glimpse of the brilliant sun of freedom.

ALL
Cliché! Cliché!

AGITATOR
All right, then, kill me because of the cliché!
Don't forgive me. Help me!
The scaffold's my last chance!
Rectify the mistakes of the past!
Edit a biography!
Reward a lifetime of struggle!

Kill me!
—WORKERS OF THE WORLD, UNITE!

THE MASKED MEN remove their
masks, turn their screens around,
revealing slogans about Prosperity,
Affluence, etc. THEY shout slogans
while crisscrossing the stage and
waving their screens and assorted
props. When the scene ends, ALL
are downstage.

    FIRST MASK
You can't get a good maid these days!

    SECOND MASK
We demand the automatic lowering
of blood pressure!

    THIRD MASK
Down with rare steaks!

    FOURTH MASK
Combat local tooth decay!

    FIFTH MASK
We demand a view of the sea!

SIXTH MASK
Teach us how to play golf!

FIRST MASK
Compulsory dieting—now!

SECOND MASK
Long live our brothers on the beaches
of revolutionary Spain!

THIRD MASK
Down with onions!

FOURTH MASK
We don't want dark meat!
We want something better!

FIFTH MASK
We want bigamy!

FIRST MASK
Tell us where to get off!

SECOND MASK
The future! Give us the future *now!*

THIRD MASK
Down with girdles!

FOURTH MASK
We want more! More of everything!

FIFTH MASK
Angst! Angst! Give us *Angst!*

SIXTH MASK
Down with elephants!

FIRST MASK
Death to death!

SECOND MASK
Blacker coffee!

THIRD MASK
We demand the instant abolition
of the generation gap!

Curtain

Scene III

The curtain rises.
Ponderous music.
From upstage, a LACKEY appears, unrolling a long, narrow carpet. HE exits. THE SOLDIER now appears upstage. HE carries a small table on which stands a tin can. HE walks just to one side of the carpet. HE sets the table down at the carpet's downstage end, directly in front of the audience, then stands next to it. THE GENERAL and TWO OFFICERS enter from upstage. THE GENERAL strides down the carpet, flanked by an OFFICER on each side and slightly behind. THE GENERAL picks up the tin can.

        THE GENERAL
This is Che Guevara.
Here he is with his mission and meaning.
Everything's in here:
his heart, his hair, his teeth—
here's his tongue—
his secrets, his medical diploma,
Das Kapital, The Communist Manifesto,
his courage, his will, and his power.
Everything. The whole greatness of Che.
That's him. Him and his glory.
Here he is, in his fatigues, his cap and his boots.

Here are his codes, phone numbers, addresses.
In these ashes lies the whole future
Che dreamed of.
Everything's turned to ashes—the essence
of the illusion that went by his name,
the bomb that never exploded.
There's no other Che Guevara.
Here he is, in person.
I've got no other proof he ever existed
except for these ashes.

THE GENERAL sets the can back on
the table. HE turns to THE SOLDIER.

THE GENERAL
You've heard that Che's dead?

THE SOLDIER
No.

THE GENERAL
You know who Che Guevara was?

THE SOLDIER
No.

THE GENERAL
Are you hungry?

THE SOLDIER
No.

THE GENERAL
Are you deprived of any rights?

THE SOLDIER
I don't understand.

THE GENERAL
Are you interested in politics?

THE SOLDIER
No.

THE GENERAL
What are you interested in?
What do you want?

THE SOLDIER
Give me back my can. It's mine.

THE GENERAL
Give him back his can. It's his.
He is a Bolivian peasant.
For whom Che Guevara fought.
He understands the value of **sacrifice**.
Che Guevara never did.

He cut short a myth. He was
a living parody of a social revolution.
The irony of heroes. The irony.
Che Guevara gave his life for his murderer.

    THE SOLDIER
It's best to aim for the head.
Some aim for the chest.
In my opinion, you'd better
go straight for the head.
If you hit a leg,
you just have to get the head later, anyway.
The arm's no good, either. The arm's really bad.
The best thing is—aim for the head.
I always do.
The heart's all right if your aim's good enough.
The head's bigger than the heart. It's safer.
So my advice is—the head.
I have always had
the best results with heads.
They appreciate it if you go straight for the head.
Sometimes you hit somebody in the arm or chest.
Then he begs you to finish him off.
That's why it's best to go for the head
right from the start.
That's my advice, anyway.

    THE GENERAL
Che Guevara never really existed.
The Communists made him up.
In Moscow they understand
the future of the Bolivian peasant.

Che Guevara is the John Wayne
for people who like that kind of thing—
a big ad for seeing South America,
a tourist attraction.
Visit South America!
Take a trip to our mountains!
Play the guerrilla!
We killed the man who killed himself.
He came for his bullet.
Cowards die, heroes live.
Nothing takes more courage than life.
Life's a good reason for being a deserter.
They offer you heroic death.
We offer you life.
Make up your mind.

FIRST OFFICER
Heroes are abstract.
They're anything but heroic before they die.
It takes death to make a hero.
There are heroic acts, but no heroes.
Heroes never believe in programs.
All they believe in is heroism,
which is nothing but a lack of solutions.
Are heroes sorry they died?
We, unfortunately, never find out.
They, fortunately, never find out, either.
Heroes are hungry for injustice.
The heroes of one nation
are the criminals of another.
Among the defeated there are heroes, too.
The world is led by dead heroes.

SECOND OFFICER
Cowards!
He gave his life; all you've got is shame.
Che Guevara wasn't persecuted by us
but by his followers.
They demanded his death.
We didn't.
They lived in the hope he would die a hero.
We didn't.
They waited eagerly for the end of the film.
Not us.

FIRST OFFICER
I've been around freedom fighters.
When they get hit, they scream.
They fight because they don't know it hurts.
They lose their illusions when you
turn them into heroes.
I beat you, and you confess.
You confess you prefer life to freedom.
Confess that you're weak and I'll help you.
Submit and I'll take care of you.

SECOND OFFICER
Kill!
Kill all those who are richer than you are!
Kill anybody more beautiful than you are!
Shoot everybody who lives in cities
more beautiful than yours.
People who don't understand you—
shoot them, too!

THE SOLDIER
No.

THE GENERAL
Are you deprived of any rights?

THE SOLDIER
I don't understand.

THE GENERAL
Are you interested in politics?

THE SOLDIER
No.

THE GENERAL
What are you interested in?
What do you want?

THE SOLDIER
Give me back my can. It's mine.

THE GENERAL
Give him back his can. It's his.
He is a Bolivian peasant.
For whom Che Guevara fought.
He understands the value of sacrifice.
Che Guevara never did.

He cut short a myth. He was
a living parody of a social revolution.
The irony of heroes. The irony.
Che Guevara gave his life for his murderer.

THE SOLDIER
It's best to aim for the head.
Some aim for the chest.
In my opinion, you'd better
go straight for the head.
If you hit a leg,
you just have to get the head later, anyway.
The arm's no good, either. The arm's really bad.
The best thing is—aim for the head.
I always do.
The heart's all right if your aim's good enough.
The head's bigger than the heart. It's safer.
So my advice is—the head.
I have always had
the best results with heads.
They appreciate it if you go straight for the head.
Sometimes you hit somebody in the arm or chest.
Then he begs you to finish him off.
That's why it's best to go for the head
right from the start.
That's my advice, anyway.

THE GENERAL
Che Guevara never really existed.
The Communists made him up.
In Moscow they understand
the future of the Bolivian peasant.

You have plenty of reason to kill.
Kill!

THE GENERAL
Yes. And you'd kill me, too, of course.
And call yourself humane.
Why? In the name of freedom?
But I am free. And what right do you have—
in the name of your freedom—
to deprive me of mine?
I don't want any other kind of freedom.
Your freedom is the misery in which we live.
Well then—in the name of the working class?
There isn't any working class any more.
Hitler's working class fought against
everybody else's working class.
It was working-class men who made up
the Gestapo, the SS, the parachute troops.
The working-class man takes any job he's
offered.

THE GUILTY MAN rushes frantically
onstage. HE glances around, sees
the tin can, grabs and hugs it.

THE GUILTY MAN
This can't go on any longer!
Why did you do it? Somebody's guilty!
Why don't you ever ask who?
I am—not mankind.

I am guilty.
I've never admitted that before.
It would be awful if everybody were guilty.
I discovered evil. I did evil. I am guilty.
I invented hunger.
I insulted Hitler. I broke a solemn promise
I'd made to Adolf Hitler.
I am a secret adviser to the American Chief
of Staff.
To the Russian Chief of Staff as well.
I killed Lumumba, dropped bombs on Vietnam,
worked people up against the Jews.
I admit to causing earthquakes, to letting
floods loose.
I am guilty.
I kept saying there was hope.
Unless you hang me, my evil will grow.
Stop killing innocent people when I'm the one
who's responsible!
Don't bother with all the others! Me! Kill me!

    THE GENERAL
Injustice is more natural than justice.
It's always there, while justice must be
invented.
And justice is only the name plastered over
a new injustice.
The greatest revolutions are those
that commit the greatest and most mistakes.

    THE GUILTY MAN
I agree. Hang me.

THE GENERAL
If you're courageous enough
to deny the existence of all hope,
you'll win the affection of the entire world.
Your future frees you
from all the illusions of the future.
Even if the world falls to rubble,
that won't stop you from proving
that your cause has triumphed.
Better that the poor and downtrodden
know that's just what they are—
poor and downtrodden.

THE GUILTY MAN
I agree. Hang me.

THE GENERAL
The technological revolution did more
for equality and social justice
than all the revolutionary movements put
together.
There *is* no equality, not even among those
who die for equality.
The poor man must hate the poor and poverty.

THE GUILTY MAN
I agree. Hang me.

THE GENERAL
Moise Tshombe wanted to buy
white freedom, white superiority,

white women, white beds.
Moise Tshombe hired whites to kill blacks.
Moise Tshombe hated black men.
An intelligent black must hate the fate
of the black man.

    THE GUILTY MAN
I agree. Hang me.

    THE GENERAL
Under every flag there are plenty of heroes.
Programs, though, don't produce heroes.
Heroes are never all on one side.

    THE GUILTY MAN
I agree. Hang me.

    THE GENERAL
But Che Guevara was alone.
He triumphed over his own secrets.
He had a plan for salvation,
only no one to tell it to.
He liked things only if others
couldn't understand them.
He was alone.

    THE GUILTY MAN
I agree.

THE GENERAL
History is written for the indifferent.
For those who will live through
a whole different history.

THE GUILTY MAN
I agree.

THE GENERAL
As for poets—they fight for the
equality of crime.
Every tyrant has his own poets
to sing of his own brand of justice.

THE GUILTY MAN
I agree. Hang me.

THE GENERAL
You don't fight for Communism.
You believe in it.

THE GUILTY MAN
I agree. Hang me.

A GROUP OF PEOPLE, including THE
OLD MAN and some partisans, enters.
A PARTISAN takes the tin can from
THE GUILTY MAN.

THE PARTISAN

Thank you, General, for having killed him.
I'm glad it was you who did it.
Thank you for having made him immortal,
brave, honorable, young.
For having saved him before he could stumble
into life's temptations.
You snatched the fruits of victory
away from him.
Thank you, General.
You cut off life at just the right moment.
You knew when to do it.
A hero's life must end
the instant his sacrifice has been completed.
Thank you for having brought his life
to a triumphant conclusion.
Heroism is the sole occupation of heroes.
Everything else is a waste of time.
Thank you, General.
Life is an animal force.
Stronger than anything else,
it will compromise every idea.
Those who manage to escape death in battle
often live on to make a mess of their lives.
You've saved another man.
Thank you, General.
Humanity will never forget you.
You are the father of a great death.
Man doesn't need freedom.
He needs a cause. A free man has none.
Thank you, General.

The dead fight for ideas, the living
for themselves.
Thank you.
Kill them while they're young
and innocent.
Don't let them get old.
Thank you for the legend, the myth.
Thank you for doing everything you could.

THE GENERAL
He started it!
He started killing in a state of nerves.
It's easier to kill than to work.
With bullets he was hunting for something
he couldn't get any other way.
No one can turn the clock back.
Great ideas had their triumph ages ago.
What truth are they looking for?
Everything that's true was true ages ago.
Che Guevara is an illusion.
It took a century for your clichés
to give birth to one man.

THE OLD MAN
No truth but illusion.
No experience but illusion.
Every experience, a suicide.
A man with hope can't be a revolutionary.
No man is happy.
Today that can be proved by statistics.

All proposals for making men happier
have been tested and junked.
The world can't be helped by wretches
who accept life as it is.
Life makes sense: we always start from scratch.
Nobody ever inherits unhappiness.
One man's old age can't be another's youth.
Old age is hopeless—
artificially maintained by pills,
injections, diets, myths.
Knowledge comes too late.

THE GUILTY MAN
You don't know anything yet.
You haven't been beaten yet.
You haven't been betrayed by your best friends
yet.
You haven't been abandoned by your loves yet.
You don't know a thing yet.
You'll return from your battle without health,
passion, ideals, joy.
Even if you win, you'll come back defeated.
History repeats itself. You know that.
You will lose your pride, honor, courage,
your place among your people.
You will become cowards and traitors.
There is no justice, no freedom, no future.

The lights go down.
Figures can just barely be seen.
Dramatic music.

In the semidarkness, full of shadows,
The Ecstasy begins.
ALL participate in this.

>   ALL
> Long live Che Guevara!
> LONG LIVE THE DEATH OF CHE GUEVARA.
> Every life is better than any death.
> THERE ARE DEATHS THAT ARE WORTH MORE THAN ANY LIFE.
> Long live the best.
> THE BEST GO ON LIVING.
> Long live triumph.
> Triumph and victory!
> EVEN OUR ENEMY'S VICTORY IS A VICTORY.
> To be victorious is to be righteous!
> Long live the freedom to choose slavery!
> LONG LIVE THE RIGHT TO SURRENDER!
> Long live equality.
> Long live inequality!
> Long live our tyranny! Long live our misery!
> Long live our discontent!
>
> WE WILL DEFEAT VICTORY!
> One can only lose honorably!
> HANG ON TO YOUR ENEMIES; YOU'LL NEED THEM.
> You'll look for enemies, but won't find them.
> IF WE CAN'T HAVE JUSTICE, WE'LL PERFECT INJUSTICE.
> If truth wins, we'll fight against truth, too.

HE RECEIVED A DIPLOMA FOR A PERFECT DEATH!
Lucky are the ashes in the other world.
LET'S CHANGE GODS.
Change gods, but leave faith alone.
GIVE US A CAUSE, AND WE'LL FIND A WAY!
No period in history has a future.
TELL THE FAT THAT THEY'RE SKINNY, AND YOU'VE GOT AN ARMY.
Heroes believe they'll attend their own funerals.
FAME BY DEATH IS PROHIBITED!
Fertilize the fields with your own ashes.
AN OLD MAN'S VIRTUE IS HIS LAST DECEPTION!
An old man's past was only his youth.
No revolution is the final one!
THE DEFEAT OF VICTORS IS THEIR REAL GLORY!
The murder of murderers is for victors only!
DE GAULLE LED THOSE WHO HATED HIM!
Stalin betrayed only his followers.
REVOLUTIONS ARE DEAD, REVOLUTIONARIES STILL ALIVE!
Down with the keepers of the ashes
of extinguished revolutions!
EVERYONE FIGHTS FOR JUSTICE—THAT'S WHY IT FAILED!
Don't trust the dead senses of living corpses!
LONG LIVE EGOISM, THE FATHER OF LIFE!
Long live the courage of egoism!
LONG LIVE YOUR CONQUERORS!
Down with happiness! Long live hope!

THE MAN WHO FORBIDS is spotlighted.
Quiet.
The rest of the stage in
complete darkness.

>THE MAN WHO FORBIDS
>No more surprises. Now you know everything.
>Surprise is forbidden.
>And no questions, either. (You've got all the answers.)
>You've experienced every experience—
>heard the unheard of.
>Go home. You know everything.
>A miracle has won.
>That's the way you should live from now on.
>That's the new life.
>Have courage. We are starting from scratch.
>No new proofs, no secrets.
>Everything clear as daylight.
>We've reached the end.
>No complaints.
>We are confronted with a blank wall.
>The show is over. Don't hope. There's no hope.
>Hope is forbidden and everything abolished,
>and nothing will ever be solved again.
>Everything is solved already.
>No more putting it off.
>This is the last, the final hour.
>No one owes anything to anybody.
>Everybody's got more than they can ever pay back.
>Don't wait.

There's nothing to wait for.
We've got it already. Waiting's forbidden.
Everything's been said. Nobody can be surprised.
Everything we'd been waiting for
has already happened.
Those who wanted the truth—they have it.
No more questions.
This is the end.

On the opposite side of the stage,
THE GIRL is spotlighted.

  THE GIRL
Our miserable life behind locked doors
is the future our great-grandfathers dreamed of.

Our age without hope, our causeless age—
it was for this that the martyrs died.

And until today—since time began—
nobody's ever had a happier future.

But the future will come. By day or by night.
When we've all died for it.

The spotlight goes out.
THE GIRL vanishes.
THE MAN WITH THE CROSS enters.

  THE MAN WITH THE CROSS
Who was looking for this cross?

Won't anybody take it? Nobody wants it?
All right. If *you* don't want it,
somebody else will. It's silly
to postpone it, though.
You might just as well take it now.
I'll leave it right here.
You can't avoid it anyhow.

HE waits for a reply, then disappears
in the dark.
Darkness and silence.
The sound of the *Internationale*.
Light comes up. THE MOTHER, holding the tin can, advances. Behind
her, large picture posters drop down,
suspended from above. Pictures of
Prometheus, Icarus, Christ, the first
man who tried to fly with wings, Stevan
Filipović, Yuri Gagarin—their arms
all pointing upward as if longing to
fly.
THE MOTHER speaks sometimes to
the tin can, then out to the audience.

      THE MOTHER
I curse every freedom won by the death
of those who fought for that freedom.
I curse every justice won at the price
of the injustice done him.
I curse the life that follows his death.
I curse the future without him,
and the hungry, the poor,

the downtrodden for whom he died.
I curse the man who will take his place.
I curse all hope and all victories.
Shame on all the survivors.
Let being alive be the greatest shame of all.
I curse his memory,
the idea that killed him,
the flag under which he fell.
I curse faith in victory,
the fate of all heroes,
the glory of the dead.
I curse the life that gave up on them.

Curtain

RANDOM TARGETS

ON YUGOSLAVS

Yugoslavs earn more than they produce and spend more than they earn. How?

It's easy. With a magic wand they simply pull out of a hat whatever the modest circumstances of the present epoch cannot offer them.

The bulk of their money they spend on cigarettes, the rest on newspapers. From the remainder they buy:

Pianos, aquariums, fountains, villas, cars, necklaces, paintings, monkeys, horses, vineyards, fur coats, farmhouses, and views of the sea, antique furniture, antique violins, antique clocks, old paintings, old coins, old maps, old weapons, old skeletons, rare stamps, rare firms, rare samples, rare books. They buy friends, mistresses, witnesses, colleagues, war comrades, and life stories; they travel to the most beautiful and the most distant parts of the world; and when they die they are buried under second-hand tombs hewn from the most expensive stone.

Whatever's left over, after these items are paid for, is put into savings accounts.

Staggering!

The Yugoslavs have obviously disengaged themselves from their state, from its problems and hardships, and ceased to be victims of its subjective and objective weaknesses.

The state is constantly experiencing some sort of scarcity: dinars, dollars, credits, prospects, solutions. On the other hand, Yugoslavs have these things, and more —in their savings accounts.

Thus not by virtue of any scientific or political prognosis, but, rather, through the survival instinct of a vital mentality, the state will wither away, and the people will survive, healthy and alive, beautiful and gay.

Good for them!

Besides: wasn't that the goal of all our efforts and struggles?

We have been witnesses to a variety of crises: in the theater, in exports, in football, in social security, in the coal industry, in education, in the family. Never have there been so many crises!

But these are the abstract crises of newspaper columns, conferences, doctoral dissertations, and scientific gatherings. In practice—for Yugoslavs—there are no crises!

Yugoslavs are finally free. They've been released from their traditional complex, taken a deep breath, and now they're simply grabbing like mad.

Thus on this volcanic ground of eternal rebellions and illegal activity, a new illegal movement is in full swing—for happiness, for a home with a garden full of flowers, for a bathroom full of tiles, for pep pills and deodorants. The less there is the more there is, the less they give the more they take.

Science is lagging, the economy is lagging, statistics are lagging. But no one can keep up with the growth and prosperity of the Yugoslavs.

Children can't wait to be born; that's how far we've come! There are now several hundred candidates for the twenty-millionth Yugoslav. Nothing is more beautiful or promising than to be a Yugoslav.

You've read about it in the newspapers: the

number of people claiming to be Yugoslavs is rapidly mushrooming. We hear from them in Austria, Italy, from all over the globe.

The time has passed when the enemy could deride Yugoslavia because its personal income was relatively low. We beg your pardon, but in Yugoslavia nobody lives on personal income. That propaganda weapon is obsolete.

Yugoslavs work for a salary, and they live on . . . What do you live on, dear reader?

Per diems, separate living allowances, bribes, tips, grants, vegetable gardens, poultry, half for you—half for me? You rent out a few rooms, take a trip to Trieste, and another to Sofia? Councils, commissions, analysis, interpreting, extra tuition, extras on extras? You copy, you edit, you recommend? You do favors, and allow a few to be done for you in return, eh . . . ? Admit . . . you have an aunt in America, an uncle in Australia, a sister-in-law in Sweden? You economize on food? You turn the old inside out to look like new? Oh! You sell houses for demolition or is it grave sites or drivers' licenses, perhaps? You sold your house and got a rent-controlled apartment from your firm? In wholesale shops you steal retail? Or vice versa? You keep cigarettes under the counter until the prices go up? You sell out the property of a former co-operative farm?

You're doing something, no doubt about it. How else would you live, you and your canary and the piano tuner and the housekeeper and the masseur and the dog, and all those others you lug on your back?

ON FREEDOM

For our country freedom is not a great tradition, but, rather, an unfulfilled dream. We've exhausted our passion for freedom in the struggle to get it.

We believed that freedom meant delivering speeches on freedom, promising freedom, erecting monuments commemorating the struggle for freedom.

We wrote freedom in capital letters and pictured it as a large gathering celebrating freedom to the accompaniment of music, the waving of banners.

We've equated freedom with the struggle for freedom. We thought that we were all dreaming about the same freedom, the same bread, the same clothing, the same song, the same woman. We wanted freedom that would liberate us from our own thoughts, worries, and work.

Freedom is not an official holiday. Freedom is not one day a year. Freedom is not the thought of freedom. Freedom is not one freedom.

Freedom is not a huge, unified, prescribed guaranteed freedom. Freedom is not a holy illusion. Freedom is a mixture of small and different freedoms.

Experts on freedom are not sure whether the population is prepared to accept this quantity of freedom. Freedom came considerably earlier than was anticipated. The future has, so to speak, just begun, and freedom is already in full swing. Freedom is becoming increasingly dangerous.

Those who yielded to freedom's temptations are afraid. Such freedom surpasses their notion of freedom;

it crops up in the most unexpected places. Freedom is hard to control, impossible to predict.

They find restaurant menus too elaborate, designs absurdly varied, and different species of pigeons senseless. They are baffled by the number of books. They dislike dilemmas. And there is no longer only one newspaper. One and the same thing is talked about in three different ways. The national lottery is not controlled, and people with doubtful pasts win the grand prize. The radio responds to the wishes of listeners who haven't been investigated. Bow ties are sold freely. Chaos. Witnesses attend trials. Newspapers publish corrections. Knowledge is taking over. Only facts are believed. Proof is wanted. Even truth is believed.

There are fewer freedom watchers, but more freedom. Who will protect us from freedom? What will happen to us?

There are theoreticians who maintain that too much knowledge, too much beauty, too much justice, too much freedom threatens the former great freedom that kept us warm for so many years. Our present freedom is vulgar and banal in comparison with that sacred freedom.

Many find such freedom hard to take. They are not equipped to deal with it. They don't believe in freedoms about which they have not been consulted. They are afraid of malpractice. They dream of having *their* freedom promptly executed. They favor clean business, etiquette, and regulations.

When visas were abolished, they expected the whole nation to emigrate. When the fence was taken down in front of the National Assembly Building, they were afraid the plebeians would lynch the deputies.

They think it's meaningless to choose the most beautiful girl simply because she is the most beautiful girl, the best song because it's the best, the most able manager because he is the ablest, the strongest boxer because he is the strongest. They seek the right motivation and the final purpose in everything.

Secretly, they hope for another war for freedom. They can't reconcile themselves to freedom for freedom's sake. Future and freedom are for them one and the same thing. Thus freedom will always be for them only a goal.

They prefer the fight for freedom to being free. The fight for freedom is always easier than the practice of freedom.

ON MEDIOCRITIES

At the corner, in front of the Hotel Balkan, stood a neatly dressed man distributing visiting cards.

>Petar Petrović
>Mediocrity

Some of the visiting cards were printed in French. With a vital addition:

>Petar Petrović
>Mediocrity from Yugoslavia

We were clearly dealing with a man who knew what he wanted, a member of the most wholesome element in our nation: he has a steady job, is politically stable, is a realist's realist, loyal to the core. In short, a good and pleasant man.

For a long time such men, our finest mediocrities, have been languishing in the shadow of other, "higher" values. But their time has come, and they now dare to declare themselves openly. Following a series of successes and recognized accomplishments, which they recorded before the eyes of the world, they now see no reason to be ashamed and lie low. On the contrary. A sense of solidarity is growing, and a recognition of the need for self-organization. Even in this era of unemployment, mediocrities will never be among the unemployed. Others will be arrested, exiled, marked for life, humiliated, but that is not their style.

They see films in which others act.
They watch plays in which others eat dinner.
They listen to records of others singing.
They buy books by people they've never met.
They vegetate in front of TV screens on which they never appear.
Gaze at magnificent structures in which they will never live.
Adore women who don't know they exist.
Build yachts in which they will never sail.
Produce scents that others use.
Get killed in wars started by others.

If we don't see these people at our functions, where are they? If the people have lost, who has won?
Mediocrities.
What is the secret of their success? Why are there so few recognized mediocrities?
A mediocrity must have both his feet on the ground. He must father a family. He must tolerate no dilemmas and suffer no dreams. In short—a professional.
In competitive situations he must insist on being the mediocrity. And this information must be clear from his visiting card.
It is hardly surprising that I myself have dreamed of becoming some kind of mediocrity.
I could outdo myself and rise above my potential.
All doors would be open to me. According to protocol, my name would make the most distinguished lists. I would make my parents happy. I would rise above the expectations and prophecies of my father and my teachers.

I would shock the doctors who had cured me. I would throw my friends (those with whom I'd had to repeat classes in high school) into positive despair.

I would substitute my lack of qualifications with loyalty, my stupidity with good behavior, my lack of talent with good connections, my ignorance with someone else's learned papers.

I would be concerned with the fate of the world instead of my own fate. I would worry myself sick over someone else's illiteracy rather than my own. I would mull over the problems of Peru. Disorderly in my own mind, I would try to establish order in the metropolis. I would be a true ambassador of mediocrities and fight for their interests every single step of the way.

But, alas!

ON THE ABUSE OF DEMOCRACY

There's a new catchword: the "abuse" of democracy.

In spite of all my efforts to solve this riddle, I have been unsuccessful.

How can democracy be abused?

Killing a man is not an abuse of democracy, but a criminal act. The same goes for stealing. An antistate act is not an abuse of democracy, but, rather, a crime with known legal consequences.

What, then, could the "abuse" of democracy mean?

Walking in the rain without an umbrella, being a vegetarian, a miser, being illiterate, hungry, moody, irritable? Every human has a right to be these. They can't be called an abuse of democracy.

Standing on one foot, talking nonsense, being without talent, writing bad books, writing bad poems—all these are the prerogatives of a free man. No, they're not an abuse of democracy, either.

What sort of democracy is it that no one can abuse?

Some believe democracy to be a "void" between two clear conditions.

In that void one can smoke, think of something else, write poems, make love.

Is there too much smoking, too much thinking, too much writing, and too much love-making? Are these an abuse of democracy?

There are people who can do without democracy

altogether. They believe democracy to be a luxury, affectation, fad, the right of every nonentity to think, desire, and love. As they see it, the current democracy has nothing to do with that great democracy of the remote future. Not all are entitled to democracy yet. Real democracy is anarchy. Democracy is not for everyone.

Democracy should be kept for holidays, anniversaries, and special achievements.

We must be sparing with democracy. So as not to use it up.

Democracy is for books, programs, shopwindows, and museums.

Each use of democracy is an abuse.

Democracy should not be sullied by hands or dragged along in the streets. It should not be introduced in substandard flats and underdeveloped areas. It's a sacred word, an abstract noun—no man is worthy of democracy.

Or freedom, for that matter.

The people were so eager for freedom that they wanted to eat it, to satisfy their individual appetites. They celebrated it, loved it, hated it, flirted with it, and played with it. They gave it the most unusual names.

And then came the grave pronouncement: Democracy is being abused.

Democracy exists, and it has laws to protect it. Everyone can distinguish between freedom and crime. It's easy to tell where freedom stops and crime begins.

Outside the law, democracy needs no keepers. Laws do not dictate freedom and democracy; they make it possible.

The privilege of some has become the right of

all. The old clichés—the voice of the people, the will of the people, the interests of the people—have become real.

Democracy is chaste. Healthy. Innocent. It serves nothing but democracy. Thus it is impossible to abuse democracy.

The abuse of democracy is the favorite topic of those who would abuse it most gladly. Of those who do not recognize views, tastes, moods, and interests outside their own.

Can there be too much democracy?

Well, there are people who still think that too much democracy inevitably leads to catastrophe. Which can be delayed by the old injustice, by crime, by wars, and by bombs. All this—for the good of humanity.

ON ISSUING STATEMENTS

It's better to work badly and express oneself properly than the reverse.

You may discover a cure for cancer, but if you fail to proclaim it as yet another blow to the power of darkness, to ignorance, to reactionary forces in general, you might just as well not have discovered it at all.

Don't discover anything, but do speak passionately about the need for a struggle against everything—including cancer—about the need to come to grips with evil. Do that and you'll find you've suddenly been promoted to the front ranks of the fighters for progress.

Work is something you have to do constantly; it's hard. Verbal statements, on the other hand, can be made sporadically, and are a lot easier. One works out of sight, whereas verbal statements are always made before cameras and microphones. Statements make a more lasting impression than deeds. Statements make the front pages. Real achievements wind up buried in the back, if there's any space left.

We have a poetess of tender heart and small talent who hasn't missed a single important date to remind us that our homeland spreads from Maribor to Djevdjelija, and that we should never forget the unforgettable.

We have a commentator who for years has signed his name to official statements, reports, bulletins, and other people's words. For this devotion to other people's thoughts he is handsomely rewarded and highly respected. There's no danger of his using his head. That's not part of his job.

His opinion never deviates from official statements. His mistakes are never his own, because, after all, his thoughts aren't, either.

One's own opinion is always an adventure, a risk, an unremunerative business.

Supporting other people's opinions is the most lucrative kind of professionalism.

Of course you love your country, your mother, and freedom. But why haven't you said so publicly? You think it's taken for granted, that it's beneath you to peddle your emotions, that it's shameful to get an apartment in exchange for such a public statement.

However, nobody believes you. Others make statements you don't. You keep quiet. Taste? Dignity? Intelligence? Those are your reasons for holding your tongue? Impossible.

Make a statement! It's simple.

As for explaining why you shy away from such an easy occupation, that's hard. Your stubbornness puts you on the defensive.

How will you ever know what you think if you don't make a statement?

You cure people, but don't explain how. You write books, but don't tell us what they're about. You engage in scholarship, but where's the political orientation? You contribute to the glory of this country, but where are you at all the patriotic clambakes anyway?

We've equated statements with opinions. Those who make the right kind of statements think right. There's no other logic.

For our work we receive salaries, but for our statements we can get social recognition. Our work gets scribbled down in our notebooks; our statements published in biographies.

A personal opinion proves absolutely nothing. Make a statement that other people's thoughts are yours, too—everything will be clear. How and what one thinks doesn't matter. What counts is what one says.

One can only think in one way: following one's moral principle. But public statements, public pronouncements, they admit a multitude of views and a flock of moral principles. It all depends. This is why statements are fundamentally infallible.

The more primitive your statement, the more sincere and convincing you sound.

It's taken for granted that people say what they think. Thus, speaking has the edge on thinking. Thinking without speaking has become suspect.

Consequently, one man who verbalizes is always in charge of three who keep quiet.

Those who make statements are equated with progress. Each word and gesture is considered a contribution to the struggle. These sentimentalities become the pearls of the epoch.

Well, here's the recipe:

If you want some peace in this life and a big reputation fast, climb on some podium, hug the microphone like a long-lost brother, and proclaim some beautiful and inspiring thought.

Do this and, though you may do little for your people, you could hardly do more for yourself.

ON BACKWARDNESS

In this day and age backwardness has become fashionable. To be backward is to be stylish. The civilized look upon the backward with envy. They are the bulwarks of progress. They are synonymous with health. They are the *avant-garde*.

The backward cannot regress. They can only go forward. The backward can take only large strides.

Only the backward have a future.

Only the poor have any hope of being rich. The rich are already rich.

And just as the shabby have more beautiful dreams than the chic, only the enslaved can still dream of freedom.

Thus the superiority of the backward rests on firm foundations. Their future is altogether certain. For they will fashion their future on the past of the civilized, without repeating the obvious errors and blunders.

Hungry and barefoot, full of dreams and energy, the backward will now experience the nostalgic moments of our past. Our most beautiful memories are about to become their reality.

They need no science fiction in their leisure hours. They dream of forks, wheels, irons, their first newspaper, the discovery of film.

They are hungry for things with which we are satiated.

What wonderful excitement, what glorious hunger and curiosity!

Fortunate are the backward, unfortunate those who are not.
Fortunate are those who still seek justice, freedom, and equality. They still have a chance of being courageous, honorable, and celebrated. They are about to have their own poets!
With our experience behind them, they will stage more brilliant revolutions, fight more spectacular wars.
Their Napoleon will be taller. Their Alexander the Great will live longer. Their Brutus will not kill Caesar.
Unfortunate are those who have reached their goal, for they are without a goal.
The free will rot in the immutability of freedom. Satiated with happiness, they will turn to unhappiness.
While the primitive idealize the good, the emancipated wearily search for a new face of evil.
The civilized fill their cemeteries by suicide, the backward by malnutrition.
The rich tell the poor that happiness is not in being rich, but the poor won't listen. Those who have clothes remove them. Those who have no clothes put them on.
Every crumb is a holiday, a step into the future.
The civilized look at the backward on small and large screens and are puzzled by the coldbloodedness that seems to lead nowhere. They would gladly leave their seats and join the game. But it's too late. Everyone can do his bit only once. Nothing can be improved retroactively. One can only go forward, and the backward are doing it.
Let's be good to the backward. Perhaps they will give us a slice of their hunger and a sip of their thirst.

ON SUSPICION AND SILENCE

A murderer kills, a thief steals, and a traitor betrays.

This is simple common sense.

However, there are people who, having settled with all known thieves, murderers, and traitors, find these simple definitions inadequate. So they adopt a sort of uprightness and devotion that condemns the rest of the population. They mistrust, suspect, doubt, eavesdrop, look for hidden meaning, guess other people's thoughts, look in their eyes, palm-read, look for ulterior motives, interpret dreams, and read between lines.

They see themselves as an isolated elite in a sea of dark intentions, possible murders, inexorable enemies, future criminals, potential assassins, hereditary reactionaries, indigenous transgressors.

For a murderer is anyone who cannot prove he hasn't killed anyone. A thief is anyone who may steal. A traitor is anyone who may betray.

They know of people who are tempted to kill, who might steal, and who are ready to betray.

They find those who hesitate, postpone, and procrastinate even more dangerous than those who have already committed criminal acts.

They've turned gray from pointless waiting; they've become ill from suspicion and deaf from eavesdropping. Their nervous system is being shattered by the uncertainty with which innocent people torture them.

To their horror, rivers continue to flow peacefully, cherry trees blossom, children are born, students graduate from school, chimneys smoke, the years come and go.

To their astonishment, killers almost invariably turn out to be people they never suspected of anything.

How wonderful it would be if their dreams were fulfilled!

They would have complete control over this game of honor, devotion, and fair play. And they themselves would determine who among them was the supreme slanderer.

Following this unpleasant introduction, allow us to ask one more unpleasant question: Who has the worst opinion of the society he lives in?

Since we don't know who thinks what, it's assumed that those who speak up have the worst opinion, because their opinion is the only one we are familiar with. They are the people who use big words, offer criticism, express opposing opinions.

The most loyal are those who don't talk. And when they talk, they don't say what they think.

When they are kindly disposed, they advise those who do talk to come to their senses, to be reasonable, to shut up, to grasp where they are living before they are swallowed up by the darkness.

People who say what they think don't believe that because they say what they think they will be swallowed up by the darkness, or they'd be silent.

People who talk are afraid of judges and prisons and everything they say; they talk because they think it necessary and permissible. They believe that stupidity and hypocrisy are the exclusive rights of the people. They think that by speaking openly about the problems of society they neither gain nor lose. They believe that to make mistakes and to have illusions are human and permissible.

Those who keep silent do so for a reason. They are rewarded by society for knowing and being silent. It's a mutual understanding. People who are silent live outside of their time; they are concerned with themselves; they behave as if they were on the moon.

For them every government is the same. They doubt that any society needs justice and freedom. They are convinced that freedom and justice do not exist. They admire the courage and madness of people who say what they think. They are stunned by so much blindness, imprudence, and stupidity. They believe they will be held responsible for every honest word they utter. In short, they have the lowest opinion of society.

Those who speak up think their lack of fear is the greatest mandate granted any society. This naïve trust society reciprocates with mistrust.

Sharp criticism is the most beautiful ode to society. These odes are full of childlike naïveté, innocence, and purity, contemporary in character and, consequently, unacceptable.

Perhaps those who are silent are right. Their experience testifies to it. No one has ever been asked to answer for his silence. The black thought that was never expressed is rewarded. Paradoxically, those who are concerned with eternity are rewarded in the present. They see their silence as the high point of courage.

Consequently, those who have made the greatest contribution to their time most often become its victims. This misunderstanding is the secret greatness of those who speak up, and the secret misery of those who are silent. The person who hasn't made a contribution to his own time cannot make a contribution to eternity. There is no eternity! Only the present. The debt that the present incurs is settled many times over by the future.

ON EXPERIENCE

The world may have little else, but it does have experience. Experience enjoys a position of the greatest respect. Experience is synonymous with maturity and wisdom. In any argument experience has priority over the finest logic. Experience is the best school. Experience is true. Experience is great. People turn to experience for advice, prescriptions, solutions. Experience teaches us, comforts us, warns us.

And yet, in spite of the honors bestowed upon it, experience is useless and unnecessary. No one has ever been able to make use of anyone's experience, not even his own. Experience is old and bitter. Experience is glum and tough.

The world does not need the experience of the old, but the illusions of the young. The world has survived not on truths but on illusions. The world would disintegrate if it were not for the inexperienced.

Not recognizing experience is a condition of man's survival.

Experience clearly and unequivocally illustrates that man is not by nature happy. Science can prove this mathematically, numerically, and graphically. As experience grew, so did evil. Every sincere proposal for human happiness has been checked out, rejected, and junked.

Experience tells us to be afraid, to be cautious, not to believe.

Experience instructs us not to sin, not to repeat mistakes.

However, what this world needs is not experi-

ence, but inexperience—young people who are not influenced by arguments, who don't know that history repeats itself, who are deaf to facts and blind to the obvious.
    Humanity survives only because man is born without memory.
    Life needs those who would go insane if they knew everything; those who would kill themselves if they were aware of everything.
    No one has ever proved anything to anyone. Everyone must make his own way through life and his own share of illusions. The whole point of life is that we always live it from the beginning. No one has ever taken over anyone's unhappiness. One man's old age cannot be another's youth. One person's experience is not another person's law. One cannot learn from anyone's experience.
    If everything were clear we wouldn't need life. Clarity is death. Too much learning will smother struggle. Accomplishment must precede experience. The unclear and ambiguous should be exploited before it becomes clear, simple, and obsolete.
    Experience stifles life, cancels hope, erases faith. Experience is a series of tragic situations proving that life is senseless, threatening those who disregard it in the name of happiness and beauty. Experience cannot put together what it destroyed when it was inexperienced. Experience repents every mistake and imprudence, but fortunately it does so too late.
    Experience tells us that we can only repeat what others have lived through for centuries. However, before we accept this we celebrate great victories of which humanity is proud, but which experience records later as useless sacrifice.

We have inexperience to thank for humanity's progress. Everything we are proud of was accomplished by men before they became experienced.

Accomplishment is a victory over experience, in defiance of all rules.

This is the meaning of experience.

ON SUCCESS AND FAILURE

The secret of success is best known to those who haven't succeeded. They know all the roads to success. They simply haven't made up their minds which one to take.

They think success is largely a question of manipulation and deception. Through women or by demagogy. Or perhaps by attacking the government at just the right moment.

But when the unsuccessful finally decide to move, they are quickly rounded up and compromised. This makes the injustice all the greater. Their honesty always betrays them. Those who try the hardest never succeed. Those who don't give a damn do. Those who don't deserve anything get to the top. None of them ever succeed in proving they got there honestly. Mankind is thus divided into two classes: those who have made it and those who haven't. The former are frauds; the latter, victims of honesty and misunderstanding.

This is where the struggle with injustice takes root.

Is it true that every beautiful woman is a whore?
Every successful writer a plagiarist?
Every free-thinking man a paid provocateur?
Every biography only a part of the real story?
Every achievement a put-up job?
Every situation staged?

Beautiful women deserve no credit for their beauty. It comes naturally.

A happy man can't come up with a single genuine explanation for his happiness.

They've done nothing for their success. Whatever they've accomplished could have been accomplished just as well by anyone else, if only they had been talented or beautiful or et cetera.

Success is a matter of chance. A rabbit is fast, but for him to take credit for his speed would be preposterous.

Success is an affront—one man insulting all others.

The successful should be ashamed. Instead, they are proud. And they go around making statements such as:

It's easy to be poor.
To be dumb and silent.
Ugly and innocent.
To be old and withdrawn.
Untalented and modest.
It's easy to be what one is.
To be a miser and on a diet.
A horse and a vegetarian.
A suicide and courageous.
Jobless and hungry.

So they talk, making free use of their talent, intelligence, and courage. They stick together. They have no heart. They take everything that's coming to them.

This tyranny can be countered only by another tyranny. All beauties will be declared whores, talented writers will be pronounced hacks, and free-thinking citi-

zens spies. The countertyranny will lie, set traps, improvise, invent, add little details, embellish. . . .
    And more.

ON THE YOUNG

Can anything be more hypocritical than the popular concern over the outrages of youth?

As if you've got your own life under control, and now you can afford to worry about someone else's? As if young people were responsible for what we've got now? Why are they such a good target for your frustrations? Are they to be blamed for having found the world in this condition?

If one were to listen to you, one would think you'd discovered a cure for death but have concealed this cure from the young. That would solve your problem and prevent them from taking the world out of your hands.

But you have no such cure, and their future is your future. If you are on the wrong side of youth, what will your future be?

Who will give you increased pensions?

Who will build better homes for the aged, better hospitals? If you go on like this, you will lie in hospitals your grandfathers built for your great-grandfathers!

Who will help you across the street?

If they don't help you out, you will spend your old age in the beds you made yourselves.

You fight all the time because you think you will always win. If you accepted inevitable defeat, you would be less aggressive. Youth will win, you know! It always does.

You are weak and old and defeated.

But you still act as if you'll have the last word.

If floods and earthquakes strike us, who will lend you a hand?

You have defeated the enemy, but not your own people.

You behave as if all this belonged to you.

You will ride on this same railway for the rest of your life if they don't build you a better one.

Who will pay your debts?

Creditors will chase you to your graves if the young don't get to work and pay off your debts for you.

What have you done to deserve their respect? Are you thinking of your future?

You will wait in waiting rooms. If they reject you, who will receive you?

Who will change your laws, prohibitions, and regulations?

You'll never see better days if they don't bring them.

You'll drink the worst wines, wear the worst clothes, see the worst films—if they don't make things better. Did that ever occur to you?

You behave as if you had perfected everything.

You think you invented progress. You ask the newborn where they were when you were in the trenches.

Is that the way to treat those who will someday lead you out of blind alleys?

You think the world will end with you.

Do you know how far you can go? Do you realize in whose hands your fate is? Is that the way to treat those on whom you depend so much?

Poor you! You'd like to perpetuate the ideals that you yourselves have abandoned.

You are still writing books about yourselves.
You offer them primers; they read newspapers.
You opened your borders, but only the highly skilled left. The unemployed stayed at home.
For a long time you didn't acknowledge the existence of anything before your time. Now you are horrified at the thought that life might go on after you.
This generation, too, will evoke young Marx someday. What will you do then? You will be bored to death with quotations.
You've done everything you could to promote contraception, but it's too late. There are more children now than ever.

IN THE INTERVAL

There was a time when students were expelled from schools for their progressive thinking. That was marvelous. You came home and proudly told your parents: I was thrown out of school!

Those were strange times.

Today your progressive thoughts have triumphed. And who could possibly believe in the victory of backward ideas?

Today it's impossible to be expelled from school for being progressive. If you are expelled, it's for poor marks or bad behavior. Ideas are never mentioned.

If you are persecuted, you must be guilty!

Today progressive ideas can bring you nothing but advancement.

At one time men lost their lives because they were ahead of their time. Today that's out of the question; no one can march ahead of his time. At best, a few miserable remnants can trail behind.

At one time people were burned, banished, and marked for life. That didn't always mean they deserved such punishment. On the contrary: in many cases, it was the punishment that brought them the glory that we attribute to their deeds.

In our day people can only blame themselves for getting into trouble with the authorities.

At one time they could blame others and thus attain eternal martyrdom. If they are persecuted today they must be standing in the way of democratic development. Many wish they could be persecuted as well-intentioned anarchists. But even that's impossible. They are persecuted as reactionaries, and who can object to that?

Everyone is against war, injustice, racial discrimination, tyranny, poverty, inequality, interference in the internal affairs of another country, colonialism, our murky past, ignorance, darkness, and unhappiness.

Everyone is for peace, freedom, independence, justice, equality, democracy, progress, brotherhood and unity, a more beautiful and happier future.

Our people have been loyal for so long that disloyalty is a strain on them. Loyalty has become second nature. They are loyal spontaneously, nonchalantly.

From overuse, words have lost their meaning.

Courage was once a betrayal of cowardice, health a betrayal of illness, beauty a betrayal of ugliness, youth a betrayal of old age. But that isn't so any longer.

At one time progressives were those who refused to make use of existing freedoms and looked for those that did not exist. Today such people would be considered counterrevolutionaries, and the counterrevolution is no longer a revolution.

The time has come when no one recognizes the unrecognized, because if they are unrecognized it's their own damn fault. The person who lives best is also the most intelligent. Triumph cannot err. No defeat is so great that it can't be considered a victory.

Today one is paid for one's anger!

The sharper the text the more they pay you. Attacks bring the highest price. Since one can always write more bitingly, it means one can live still better. Just close your eyes and lash out at everything! Your poor, naïve old mother frets that something might happen to you as a result, and you go to your accountant to find out how much the person you attacked paid you for the attack.

If you go beyond the acceptable limit, you are indeed a fool. If you were to immolate yourself in the name of the hungry poor, they'd be the first to call you an idiot. If you have food yourself, why the sacrifice? Today people are told at what time, in what place, and why they should be indignant! Spontaneous indignation is considered uncivilized and deserving of punishment. Stupidity is punished, not courage. Respect breeds contempt. A man will respect you only if you hold him in contempt!

This nation has no national anthem!

Exaggeration became impossible. A challenge for a madman!

Some still accept the position of being misunderstood and unrecognized. For this they receive state welfare. It's impossible to be persecuted in the name of a sacred cause, because it has already been done. It's impossible to sacrifice oneself for the future, because a cure for the future has already been discovered.

Society sponsors competitions to reward the sharpest attacks, which it needs for entertainment.

Everyone now understands that unless one succeeds in this life, one never will.

If you have any brain at all, coupled with a sense of proportion, your success is guaranteed.

Those who wish to make a sacrifice look for a motive in the classified ads.

This is what distinguishes our own times from all others—which is why some think that we don't even live in a time of our own. That we live in an interval between times.

ON COMMON SENSE

Humanity's highest ideals have always been freedom, justice, and equality.

No one is against human happiness, and yet the struggle for basic human ideals has been with us since our beginnings and will remain with us until doomsday.

The struggle for justice continues. One can still be a revolutionary by fighting to free the innocent, a democrat by allowing for opposition opinions, a leader by promising justice.

No leader has ever promised his people injustice or lawlessness. No one has ever given his life for the wrong cause, and yet justice hasn't won.

Since time immemorial men have been fighting for ideals that no one has opposed.

How does one fight for justice if no one is against injustice?

The problem appears to be with the fighters themselves. The injustice is in us, not in others.

Everything is clear, and everything is unclear.

Common sense has formulated what is clear. What is unclear results from a lack of common sense.

It is generally assumed that the victory of common sense does not require a struggle, because common sense is taken for granted. However, the struggle for common sense is, in fact, the only struggle people are really engaged in. The struggle for common sense is synonymous with the struggle for progress. Every revolution was conducted, and every life lost, for the victory of common sense, but common sense has not won. It did not win because man is limited and cannot overcome his limitations.

Not to be limited, to be normal, is synonymous with genius, the privilege of philosophers and wise men.

It is almost impossible to be normal and not make history. Even a drop of common sense insures fame and eternity. Even history is made of achievements that every school child is familiar with. In terms of history the ideas of contemporary leaders are stale and outmoded, but in terms of our times they are dangerous and revolutionary. Those who, in terms of common sense, are fit to become criminal-court justices are hailed in this time of madness as the stars of liberalism and democracy.

There is still a place for fighters for freedom of the press, freedom of art, freedom of opinion and speech. These basic human rights were formulated hundreds of years ago, and it is hard to accept the fact that they have not been realized yet. However, they haven't. One goes through history treading the paths of ancient programs and slogans. There are no original ideas and no original causes.

Promises best formulate what man still lacks. Nations that appear to be free are promised freedom, and those that are believed to be rich are promised bread.

One can only promise things that aren't there and awaken hope for things that one wants but doesn't have. You don't promise freedom to the free, employment to the employed, independence to the independent!

All promises are in fact accusations against tyranny and injustice. They are a cry, repeated endlessly, for the victory of common sense.

It appears that humanity will meet its end without ever experiencing the triumph of common sense. Man seems to lack sufficient common sense to realize eternal ideals, born of intrinsic needs and rights. It is hardly an accident that we refer to freedom and justice as ideals. These ideals are synonymous with common sense. Ideals remain—ideals.

The end is approaching, yet the gap separating humanity from common sense grows wider, and its victims more numerous.

ON NATIONS

Are at least two nations essential to the existence of one?
Can one viable nation be made out of several dubious ones?
Can two nations give birth to a third?
Is there a small nation without a heroic past?
Is there enough freedom for all nations?
Is there enough time for each nation to win one great victory?
Can we agree on the world's worst nation?
Are two nations required to have brotherhood and unity at one and the same time?
Can every man be the son of his people?
Is our nation better known abroad than it is at home?
What does a nation think with?
Are there two identical nations?
Is there a nation that no one ever heard of?
Is a nation that continuously changes regimes fickle?
Is there an anti-nation nation?
Who will erect a monument to a nation?
Why does a nation that never borrowed in the first place have to pay back debts?
Are there nations and nations?
Are there retired nations?
Are there any worries greater than national worries?
(When two sides fight, which one of them represents the nation?)
Are there ideal nations?
Can a nation be invented?
Does a nation last longer if kept in a cool, dry place?
Can one resign from a nation?

Can one die a natural death for one's nation?
Is a mob a nation?
(Why do small nations always fight for equality?)
To whom does a nation pay dues?
Are there enough small nations around to secure world peace?
Without conquest, would so many nations have a glorious history?
Did monarchies have people?
How do you remain loyal to a nation that abandoned you?
Is one river enough for two nations?
Is the glory of one nation the tragedy of another?
Are there nations that misrepresent themselves?
Can a nation be greater than the number of inhabitants?
Can a cemetery be a frontier between two nations?
Can a nation start a private state?
Where were so many nations during the war?
Has there ever been a plebiscite without a nation?
What portion of a nation is not representative of a nation?
Is there a nation that isn't always in the right?

00

In one of our freedom-loving regions, in a restaurant with national specialties, a justifiably exasperated and badly served guest calls over the waiter and in no uncertain terms asks for a pencil.

He gets up from the table, and marches directly across the restaurant, and enters the men's room (WC, urinal, lavatory, latrine, water closet), henceforth referred to as 00.

He wants to relieve himself of his anger as soon as possible, to state his fury in written form, to speak his mind openly and without restraint. He is not the only one. In front of the 00 is a long line of men gnashing their teeth and sharpening their pencils to express their thoughts on all sorts of injustices, open their hearts, soothe their suffering souls.

They have been silent long enough! Now they are ready to go all the way! Everything or nothing! Necessity changes the law.

They are highly individual men: revolutionaries who cannot accept the established routine and social hierarchy, open opponents of the regime, anarchists, pedantic dogmatists, unhappy lovers, misunderstood and unrecognized poets and painters for whom this is the only congenial arena of expression. For twenty dinars they find in this confessional their place and their only chance.

Here they are all equal. Far from the city hubbub, between these four walls they can make their modest contribution to human progress and happiness.

Much of this writing is done too fast; many

thoughts are left incomplete. Others have to be let in and given a chance as well. But no one can doubt the sincerity of these outpourings. For many it is the only workroom, the only laboratory, the only podium.

We need hardly mention that man's first efforts to record his thoughts were etched on walls.

This tradition is long and brilliant. Defeated in battle, men withdrew into the 00, defending their honor to the last drop of blood.

There's no spot in the world in which human imagination has spread its wings wider, no place that has greater autonomy and integrity.

In acts of vandalism house painters and cleaning women try to destroy the work of these people. Carpenters change inscribed doors. The battle goes on. I venture to anticipate its outcome: the last door that remains in place will be enriched by the freedom-loving hands of the new tribunes.

This practice is not restricted to our population alone. It is international, and everyone is given equal opportunity.

More than once in our lifetime we have seen writing in foreign languages, strange scripts of foreign alphabets and cultures. That was our dear visitors, foreign students, honeymoon couples giving vent to their feelings. Many of these worthwhile thoughts will, unfortunately, forever remain undeciphered. Many will disappear in this singular record of impressions.

Joyce astutely remarked that the latrine is the place where men think most intensively. If a man were to think at no other time, this would be ample. As proof of this act of thought a written testimonial is left behind.

The four walls and the ceiling are treated as five pages of an exclusive newspaper, covering news from foreign politics to sports, in pages neatly organized into columns, including open letters, interviews, court sentences, comic strips, and obituaries. All of this is illustrated with familiar informal illustrations.

No police in the world have such a large collection of fingerprints.

It's a newspaper with something for everybody. Our Hyde Park. The last bastion of freedom, written in juicy popular speech, untouched by cruel editors, without censorship, without fear.

Those who think that no real polemic exists in our society should take a peek in there. They would witness a free and uncompromising difference of opinion.

I recently overheard the following remark: "I read a marvelous article in the latrine. He really let them have it! That's a good mind for you, a good mind!"

Now that is freedom of the press!

Not long ago I read the following graffito in the men's room: "Down with the King!"

Obviously, people don't think of the consequences.

Unfortunately, we are unable to appreciate the wealth we have. This unique collection is badly preserved.

So far, we have covered only the achievements of the male part of this institution, but women are probably not sitting idle, either!

THE "YES" MAN

Anything you say.
If you say so.
I agree with you.
I'll give you my version of your opinion.
I don't know what to think.
I'd do it if I knew others would go along, too.
I'm not concerned with the truth. I know who's right.
The Germans would have lost the war even if I hadn't hated them.
I'm not afraid to speak out. I'm only afraid of the consequences.
Who am I to fight for justice?
What would I have gained by getting myself killed?
Even if I'd had an opinion of my own then, it would be different by now.
It's easy to rebel; it's hard to put up with things.
I'm a progressive. I'm always for the most recent decisions.
My opportunities are unlimited. I've no opinions of my own.
What if I had an opinion of my own? What if I didn't guess right?
Everyone would be for something better if he knew that he wouldn't be worse off than he is.
Everyone would have fought if they had been sure of remaining alive.
I know better than to be the only one in the right.
What others do is good enough for me.
Be quiet until you're told what to say.
Modest people last longer.
Am I in anyone's way?

Who bothers to ask me anything?
Who am I to fight for justice?
There are lots of people brighter than I am.
Why me?
I stick to my own business.
My problem is that I keep quiet, but then there are more serious problems.
We can't all be fighters.
If I'd listened to myself, I would never have gotten this far.
If we were all heroes, who would sweep the streets?
Pay no attention to me.

ON FILM

In 1945 many things that we now take for granted were considered inconceivable. Nobody thought then that twenty years later hundreds of thousands of Yugoslavs would be working abroad. Only reactionaries would have suggested that former partisans would be picking up paychecks from German firms.

It never occurred to anybody that students would go on delivering milk from door to door, or that the sons and daughters of revolutionaries would be sent abroad to be educated. Not even the wildest imagination could have dreamed of former war criminals vacationing with wife and children in sunny Yugoslavia. Few were aware that churches and castles were part of our cultural heritage, that historically they were priceless. There were people who had returned from the future and who claimed that in that future there would be no unemployment, no illiteracy, no rigged trials. There would be no whores, bars, gambling casinos, strip-tease halls, no corruption or inequity in material things and salaries, no civil servants, fashions, ladies, servants, or street sweepers any more. Only the most callous among us could believe that we would ever be short of electricity, that our schools would ever shut down, that we would mourn the death of an American president, smoke American cigarettes, drink American liquor, chew American gum, wear Italian shoes, drink Spanish wines, buy German-made cars, sing cowboy songs.

Who could ever have believed we would have former German soldiers for sons-in-law, to say nothing of how happy we are to have them as tourists.

All that is normal today. Which was inevitable. One period in history was settling accounts with one set of illusions, the other with another set. Impossible things became plausible. No one objected. Everybody understood.

None of this betrayed the revolution, negated progress. There's no arguing with progress. All of this evolved logically and gradually, in keeping with the cruel laws of time.

New times required new slogans, new truths, new illusions. The progressive and backward are few in number. But the battle as to who is the more progressive is great.

Another time has another set of fighters, other and different accomplishments, idols, needs, experts, people. Former fighters quietly gave up many of the illusions of their time.

Who can judge a period in history?

Ascetics can't be judges, nor can their judgment be acceptable to anyone who is normal and healthy. Weight watchers can't plan menus; blind people can't be art critics; people afflicted with cirrhosis can't stamp out alcoholism; flat-footed people can't abolish athletics; the impotent can't denounce whorehouses; bald people can't set hair styles. Ascetics are responsible for asceticism.

Only healthy people can decide how much and what normal man needs.

They all accept new needs, new ideals, new views, new truths, new heroes, new causes, new programs. No one wishes to stop anything or to impose irrevocable laws. There is only one field in which some still wish to impose slavery under the same old truths and laws.

That field is art.

There are people to whom everything else is clear and normal, who accept everything new times bring; they are very constructive and flexible; they don't insist much on their illusions; they don't ask a single moral question.

A lot of things are clear to them that don't particularly need to be clear. They even accept changes that no one would blame them for if they didn't accept. Everyone would understand. However, they accept everything the new times bring—but

blindly, consistently, independently of all events, regardless of anything, contrary to facts, in spite of reality, contrary to all times and life—they wish (for example) that film remain on the level of their youth. To be a small museum of slogans, a bastion of illusions, a fortess of naïve causes, an archive of eternal youth, a cellar of abandoned principles, a safe for mirages, a refrigerator for early impressions, a consolation for reality, a refuge for beautiful dreams, an alibi and shelter for everything that had to pass long ago.

They lodge their protest against the truth in films.

They aren't interested in reality.

Only in films do they refuse to accept the new times.

Only in films do they object to reality.

Only in films do they rebel against the new government.

It's perhaps because life goes on and film remains. Film should preserve what life has abandoned. But they no longer make films about themselves, either. Alas.

A MORON'S REPLY

I'm a moron, that's true. I'm not ashamed of it, either. It's no shame, or sin, either. I may be stupid, but I'm no fool. I've been well brought up, and if I get a letter I'll reply with a letter. I'd be curious to know what *you'd* do if *you* were a moron.

I'm a moron, but let's start from the beginning.

Your invitation to a struggle against stupidity at this time is entirely unjustified. I don't think we're quite up to that yet. I may be stupid, but I'm not naïve. It's a strange thing, doctor. When things were tough, we were never divided into morons and those others. It turns out that in those days we were all intelligent.

If I'm wrong, feel free to correct me. Although I'm not stupid enough to think that just because you correct me that means I'm wrong.

What was I going to say . . . ? Oh, yes. Don't we have anything to fight these days except fools? Is stupidity really the main trouble in our society? Or is it that since we have everything else, only stupidity troubles us?

I didn't invent stupidity; I was born of a mother, too. I believe in my stupidity. It hasn't betrayed me once—not like intelligence, which betrays you all the time. Why this witch hunt? I've been stupid for thirty-eight years now, and it hasn't bothered you. We're overdoing it, doctor.

Until I got your letter I never gave my stupidity a thought. It seemed perfectly normal to me. Now you put a question mark to my life and work. Though I'm a fool, I don't deserve such treatment. I don't smoke; I don't drink; I don't chase women. Why can't I be stupid?

I went to school; I changed jobs several times. No one ever asked me if I was stupid. They asked other things, but not that.

I don't regret being stupid. There's no law against stupidity.

We've all gone far beyond the phase of stupidity you're dealing with. Stupidity doesn't stand still. We've all invested part of ourselves in that magnificent structure that you call stupidity. Stupidity's overcome all barriers. You're the only person who doesn't know that.

If we really want to get to the bottom of this thing, and since you're tempting me, I'll tell you that healthy monkeys remained monkeys, and man evolved from a sick monkey. I don't feel I'm in any way to blame for that.

Why don't you admit it: if there weren't any stupid people, how would you know who's intelligent?

That's one thing. Another is that stupidity has lots of advantages over intelligence. Let me list them from memory:

Morons aren't afraid or shy. They don't have any problems. They don't suffer from a guilty conscience, inferiority, false morals, or sentimentality. Everything's clear. Morons don't ask questions, don't expect answers. Every explanation will do; every reply is correct; every solution the only possible solution, every decision the right one.

No one's ever died of stupidity; no one's ever been hanged on account of stupidity; no one ever committed suicide because of stupidity.

Not long ago I received a letter from a moron in France. He thinks much the same as I do.

Besides, stupidity is taught in school. Stupidity is transmitted from generation to generation. Stupidity is recorded in encyclopedias. Stupidity is the center of attention. Stupidity is popular. Stupidity isn't petty.

There are anthologies of stupidity, cycles of stupidity, cyclones of stupidity, requiems to stupidity, culminations of stupidity. Stupidity is a whole branch of philosophy.

I've raised my voice a little. Injustice hurts.

Stupidity is, so to speak, my guiding principle in life.

And now tell me, if you will, what is it that the intelligent have done that's so much better than what we've done?

My very own brother is intelligent and he whines all the time. He has nothing to eat. He wears my clothes, makes love to my former girl friends, and doesn't bring back the change when I send him out to shop.

In what field has intelligence triumphed, where and when?

Don't look for my support. Stupidity is my defense.

We were stupid, doctor, long before you were born. Stupidity is older than intelligence. If the first man hadn't been stupid, the second one would never have been born at all.

Besides, only the more intelligent give in. Also, tell me: Among those who receive prizes and trophies, how many are really intelligent?

And when did you last listen to what an intelligent man had to say to you?

I'd be curious to know how to exercise intelligence in this situation. That would be utopia. Intelligence is impossible to sustain.

I just thought of one more stupid thing: Wouldn't it have been better to attack intelligence? There's less of it. You would have won easily, as usual. Great is the power of stupidity. Intelligence is a luxury. Intelligence belongs to the past. Only stupidity has a future.

What will you say to this: When was the last time a stupid man was expelled from the Academy of Sciences? Never.

You don't know what problems we've had with intelligent people. Intelligence has separated itself into exclusive groups, separated itself from the people.

The gulf between us is deep. They are ashamed of things that make us proud.

What intelligent man would ever do what morons have done? The greatest stupidities are the deeds of morons.

Besides, what would happen if morons thought? It would amount to the same thing.

If it weren't for morons, who would ever announce failures as successes with so much zeal and conviction, without any questions asked?

Let's be realistic. Try to understand us. We can't let anyone push us around. We're physically stronger, mentally sounder. Intelligence is an incurable disease.

Frankly, I see no way out for either intelligence or stupidity. By tomorrow, today will be yesterday. I see no reason to hurry. The greatest blunders are still before us. An attack on one stupid man is an attack on all of us.

Forget the notion that everyone can be stupid. One must believe in stupidities. Stupidity doesn't tolerate discouragement, insecurity, curiosity, and dilemma.

If you had by some chance hurled all those insults at an intelligent man, he would have done something stupid. Intelligence is conceited, sensitive, neurotic, vain, pedantic, sour, irritable. Stupidity is clean, simple, and natural.

I admit that when I talk of stupidity I am partial. It's too late to abandon stupidity now. We must stick it out to the bitter end.

Stupidity is not a fact. Stupidity is dreaming about conquering stupidity.

Don't be ungrateful.

Study stupidity, admire stupidity, spread stupidity. Don't make a scarecrow out of stupidity.

Besides, what do you know about stupidity? You've yet to read about the greatest stupidity.

Plant both your feet firmly on the ground. Then we'll talk openly, like men.

Give us proof of your stupidity, and I'll reveal to you the beauty, the sweep, the breadth, and the depth of unexcelled stupidity.

I'm telling you all this because I have confidence in you. I feel you're properly inclined.

Forgive me if I've said anything intelligent. I assure you, I didn't intend to.

ON PROGRESS

This is the triumph of the First Century.
This is no longer the First but the Second Century.
We aren't going to use any Second-Century methods in the Third Century.
The Fourth Century is the end of the darkness of all previous centuries.
Some people don't seem to have caught on yet that this is the Fifth Century, not the Fourth.
We are the children of the Sixth Century. We're completely free of all Fifth-Century prejudices.
The Seventh Century is far in advance of preceding centuries.
Does not the Eighth Century write *finis* to the Seventh?
A hundred years had to pass before we finally understood that we no longer lived in the Eighth but in the Ninth Century.
Let us strive to be worthy of the Tenth Century—the dream of the boldest spirits of the Ninth.
The Eleventh Century is a far cry from the bloody Tenth.
We dare not allow the Twelfth Century to repeat the mistakes of the Eleventh.
With the bloody experience of the Twelfth Century behind us, we can look forward to a brighter Thirteenth.
How long do we have to put up with this tyranny? This is the Fourteenth Century!
How long this injustice? This is the Fifteenth Century!
How long this poverty? This is the Sixteenth Century!
Down with the horrors of the Sixteenth Century. Long live the victorious Seventeenth!

The Eighteenth Century—our golden opportunity to avoid a repetition of the Seventeenth.
The Nineteenth Century—refuge at last from the terrible tragedies of the Eighteenth.
The Twentieth Century has always been, and remains to this very day, the eternal goal of humanity.

ON REASONING

Ask us whether you are well off or not.
Why are we here?
Find out from us about your future.
We alone know how hard up you are.
You don't know a thing about it.
You have to be told you are hungry.
You have accepted your poverty as a decent life.
You are unfamiliar with your life goals.
It is not altogether clear to you that some day you will be happy.
You are satisfied with what you've got.
You don't know what you don't have.
Who are you to think you can take care of yourself?
What have you done for your life?
It's up to you to decide whether you are pleased or not.
You believe you know, you think you know, how to think.
Someone else's thought has brought you to where you are.
You don't even know how to dream.
Being alive is normal for you.
The only thing you know how to do is work, and yet you never stop complaining about it.
You live from day to day.
You don't know what is awaiting you at the end.
You slept while your problems were being solved.
You've slept through the most beautiful moments in history.
The struggle for the future is being carried on against your will.
We dream dreams of a better life for you.
We speak, fight, and think in your name.

(Keep quiet while we are talking.)
No one has ever asked you a thing.
You've never heard of the future.
Had we met earlier, everything would have been different.
Don't think about your life; you'll spoil everything.
Forgive us for everything.
Until yesterday you didn't believe we existed.
If we weren't around, you'd live without us.
If it weren't for us, you'd live as you always have.
How long do we have to chastize you for your own good?
If it had been up to you, no one would have died, courageously or otherwise.
You enjoy everything.
So long as something is a possibility, you are willing to give it up.
We'll lead you to your goal.
Don't interfere.
Leave everything to us.
We'll explain everything in the end.
We don't have the time now.
Have confidence.
We haven't betrayed anyone yet.
We are here today, but tomorrow we'll be somewhere else.
Don't bother us; stay put.
Have you read anything in this field?
Your last assignment may be to commit suicide.
Believe that failure is a permanent condition.
You'll be surprised.
We don't say this for our sake.
We'll present all our victories to you.
I'll give you a ring when you've won.
You are our hobby.

MY SYSTEM OF FAILURE

>   To an adventurer,
> nonentity, nobody, desperado, dummy, charlatan, phantom, serpent, fool, skeleton, pauper, tramp, beggar, dunce, ignoramus, mediocrity, rag, rubbish, shadow, thickskin, pickpocket, cheat, swindler, brute, crud, oaf, loser, illiterate, hobo, scoundrel, rotter, do-nothing, scarecrow, dilettante, nitwit, imbecile, weakling, thickskull, driveler, moron, blockhead, half-wit, ass, from anywhere and everywhere,
> NOW THEN—FROM SUCH A
>   rare, exceptional, unexpected, exclusive, singular, isolated, unprecedented, exemplary, exotic, well-preserved, unique, authentic, independent, extravagant, characteristic, principled, strong, complex, committed, stubborn, self-conscious, superior, uncompromising, clearcut, happy, well-integrated, well-defined, and self-contained person—
>   we were able, during the last few days, at the last minute, to extract—by resorting to
>   promises, lies, cunning, trickery, special herbs, beatings, kicks in the ribs, milk and honey, electrodes, blunt objects, threats of forced labor, and a quickly improvised gallows—a confession:
>   How I succeeded in remaining unnoticed at a time when no
>   fool, dilettante, illiterate, ignoramus, dropout, amateur, phony, member, person, moron, parasite, microbe, bug, ass-licker, charlatan, scarecrow, monster, bloodsucker, vampire, pickpocket, kleptomaniac, plutocrat, scum, cow-

ard, blabbermouth, chameleon, operator, lunatic, hypochondriac, cocksman, blockhead, black marketeer, horse thief, bon vivant, antichrist, bore, slob, boor,
    who is not now
        in charge, an adviser, organ, eminence, personality, example, patron, doctor, department head, supervisor, inspector, trustee, executive secretary, honorary member, best-selling author, star, teacher, pride and joy, representative, master of ceremonies, interpreter, expert, master craftsman, maestro, conductor, guide, visionary, power, driving force, magnate, man about town, professional, aristocrat, fighter,
    or
        interviewed, photographed, asked, promoted, publicized, famous, conceited, overestimated, crazy, affected, consulted, specialized, financed, educated, fed, patted, adored, adorned, decorated, inaugurated, given a position, pushed, imposed, superimposed, supported, encouraged, accepted, paraphrased, quoted, consummated, pleaded with, elected, recommended, boosted, systematized, insured, cared for, made comfy, contented, free, celebrated, glorified, recognized, translated, emphasized, rewarded, praised;
        at a time when people do not exist who stand for nothing, who know nothing and have nothing, the man in question is indeed an exception, phenomenon, *Wunderkind*, the only possible miracle, a rare commodity, hero, a real actor;
        when it became practically impossible to avoid glory, honor, popularity, fame, visiting cards, titles, money, women, importance, rights, podium, platform, posing, admirers, place and role . . .

—one man withdrew! He shunned radio, flash bulbs, cameras, stages, receptions, premières, awards, diplomas, motives, snobs, bars, lights, gifts, depths, eternity; in short, he shunned everything.
Bravo!
The world didn't believe him. His life was feverishly analyzed, and all witnesses were cross-examined. They were looking for a needle in a haystack, for a crumb of success, the vaguest confession that could compromise him.
But they found nothing, nothing at all. There is no school, factory, institution, home for the aged, hostel, hotel, motel, hospital, clinic, magazine, report, analysis, study, list—not one that records his name.
Is it possible that such a man lived among us? Without getting the rights for which he had fought? Unbending in his exclusiveness? If he hadn't died, we would have hanged him.
Is there no application he has submitted? No résumé, no summary of qualifications?
I ask myself: Who is responsible? Who let this beast slip away in broad daylight?
Hadn't he ever made use of the most basic human rights? How could he have resisted it? How could he have resisted the temptations of our age? Every fool knows, after all, that it's easier to succeed than not to succeed.
Who is responsible for his triumph and our defeat?
We did everything we could. There's no excuse. There would have been no explanation, either, had we not extracted the dirty secret from him on his deathbed. Actually, he was fairly helpful in this, too. He felt guilty

because of what he had put us through. He wanted to die clean.

    Until yesterday the mean and the stupid gaped at the tiny helpless man on his deathbed—those without any reflex or imagination, blinding flash bulbs and reflectors, radar and microphones. The agitated world awaited the news, having been promised an explanation of the failure.

    Our hero passed his emaciated fingers through his gray hair and tried to recall. The angry mob wanted to lynch him.

    The frightened man spoke:

    It all happened rather suddenly. While I was in the shed getting firewood, *you did the job*. I am ashamed. Forgive me. Never again . . .

    And he died.

    Thus at the last minute, this one pure life was put to shame. He had managed to remain unnoticed all his life, but on his deathbed he emerged from his anonymity, entered history and became a hero of our times—our comrade.

ON THE FUTURE

Everyone waits for the future; it never comes. No time in history has ever been future. Belief in its imminent coming has not slackened, however.

Men never stop believing in victory over themselves, although their imperfection thrives only in an imperfect society. The future is the abolition of reality.

Men today are no more intelligent than their forefathers. Children are still born illiterate. The future will always be sufficiently removed in time. The ideal man is as remote now as before the last dozen revolutions. But man still believes that in the future he will defeat his own nature.

The issues are unchanging. Old injustices are being remedied under new tyrants. That's progress.

Even though they get only one chance on earth, men postpone their freedom to some future date. Every act against the present is legitimized by the future. Yet the future doesn't exist.

Gone are the days for which the greatest minds of our past fought. Gone are the days for which someone fought somewhere. Gone are the days for which we have been waiting. The future never came. Time and again the future has been crushed by the very period that we mistook for the future.

The truth is: man is not worthy of the future. The future he wants is too good for him. Thus the future remains the future, and not the present. The world is waiting for what has been. Time has run out. The language has been fully amortized. The past is in front of us.

Instead of doing what he can, man swears to accomplish the impossible. He wastes time waiting for the future.

Future generations will be born with their own future, not ours. The natural future of man, of course, is death. The concept of the future was devised as a substitute for the discredited afterlife. The future is a mirage. Time has run out, but preparations for the arrival of the future go on.

Progress doesn't exist. A thousand years from now people will live their own lives, not a better version of ours. Different things cannot be compared. The death of a man is not his past, but his future. In the past he was alive. A dead man is the present of a corpse and not the past of a dead man. Therefore, there is no time, but only a link between different things.

Innocent victims of the past believed that in the future, for which they were sacrificing themselves, there would be no innocent victims. The innocent dreamed that their innocent suffering would gain them an easy entrance into history. But nothing has changed here, either. The innocent are still victims. The guilty alone are given a trial, while the innocent are judged ahead of time.

Humanity has had an endless number of harsh reckonings with its dark, primitive, and backward past.

The prophets and visionaries do not sit still. Generations are awaiting the future that will never come. There are witnesses to that future who have come back, given us their impressions, and stampeded us into believing them. There are countless committees for the reception of the future. They have established exactly what the future will bring:

love-making will no longer require two people;
cherries will assume free form;
children will grow gold teeth;
the raven will no longer be distinguishable from
  the swan;
mountains will be taller, seas deeper;
for going to prison you will need an application
  form, two letters of recommendation, a statement that one has never been convicted before,
  and reservations;
those who feel like it will lecture in universities;
earthquakes will be used for plowing, floods for
  irrigation;
every man will publish his own newspaper;
snow will fall in the summertime;
school children will be given instruction in the
  form of gifts;
every city will be a capital city;
and the night will have daylight;
cages will have no bars;
we will all win every lottery;
all roads will lead to final goals;
everyone will be intelligent;
pain will be pleasant;
there will be no ordinal numbers;
bridges will be built first, then rivers;
we'll all have high foreheads;
thieves will give themselves up to school children;
one hundred will be two hundred;
money will be available at low cost;
questions will be superfluous;

> the moon will always be full, the sun without spots;
> we'll conquer the neighboring planets, and we'll each have one;
> (when every man has his own planet we'll give the earth to our children to play on, on weekends).

That's the way it's going to be!

This bit of guesswork will suffer no criticism. It's pretty clear who would doubt the feasibility of this project.

Those who do not believe in this future deserve no future at all.

ST. MARY'S COLLEGE OF MARYLAND LIBRARY
ST. MARY'S CITY, MARYLAND

36624